The Erotic Soviet Alphabet

РУССКАЯ АЗБУКА

из 36 букв

от А до Ижицы

акварельные рисунки художника И.И.ИВАНОВА
(1886-1924)

The Erotic

Soviet

Alphabet

Sergei Merkurov

ECHO POINT BOOKS & MEDIA, LLC

Published by Echo Point Books & Media
Brattleboro, Vermont
www.EchoPointBooks.com

Cover Design & Interior Layout by Rachel Boothby Gualco
Editorial and proofreading assistance by Ian Straus

Printed and bound in the United States of America

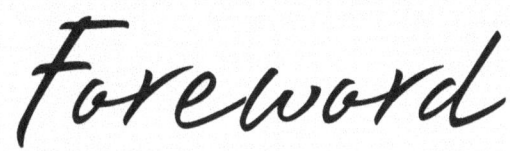

Foreword

Little is known for sure about this unusual set of burlesque prints from the early days of the Soviet Union. Likely a personal project of sculptor Sergei Merkurov's, this artwork was never formally published at the time of its creation. In fact, this edition is the first known official printing of these pieces as a collection. Merkurov is probably best known for his somewhat macabre position as the Soviet Union's most renowned producer of death masks. After studying art in Germany and Paris at the turn of the 20th Century, Merkurov returned to Russia in 1907 where he worked on numerous post-mortem masks commissioned by prominent political and cultural figures. Sometime shortly thereafter he created this set of prints, presumably influenced by his admiration for Classical Greek and Roman art.

Upon their resurfacing in the internet age, this collection of unusual artwork was unsurprisingly embraced by the blog community for its appealing blend of campy raunch, historical and cultural intrigue, and artistic playfulness. Furthermore, the air of mystery around the potential reasons for its creation adds to the appeal. An early online poster of the prints flippantly remarked that perhaps they were part of a USSR battle against illiteracy. While he may have been joking, the rumor spread like snow across the Siberian tundra and many online sources now mistakenly attribute the existence of these prints to a nation-wide education campaign. Amusing and appealing as this theory is, it is very unlikely. As those familiar with the Russian alphabet will have noticed, this book, dated 1931, contains several characters that were eliminated in the orthographical reform of 1918. If the government were to attempt to promote literacy using pornographic alphabet primers surely they would have had the presence of mind to illustrate the correct alphabet!

The inclusion of these antiquated letters also suggests that the collection may have been created prior to 1918 but for some reason left unsigned and undated until the 30s. Why would Merkurov wait over ten years to sign and date his work? Your guess is as good as ours. Perhaps it had something to do with cultural buttoning-up as Stalin's grasp tightened on the Soviet artistic community in the early 1930s (effectively ending the post-October artistic bloom). Or maybe the discrepancies are merely the result of Merkurov's personal whims or some impossible-to-fathom coincidence.

In any case, Mervurov has left us with this wonderfully naughty collection of scandalous and amusing prints. Without further ado, we'll let the art speak for itself.

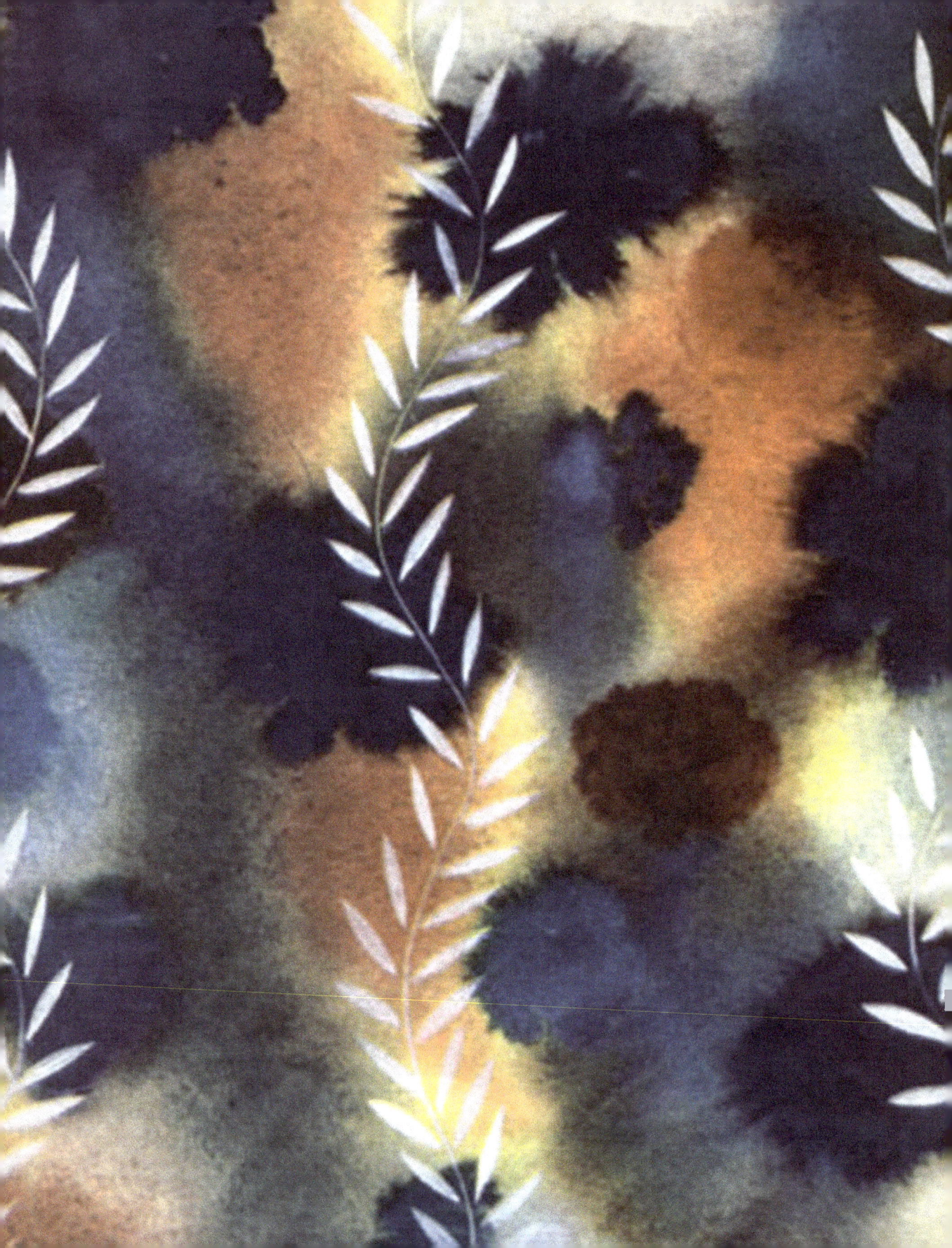

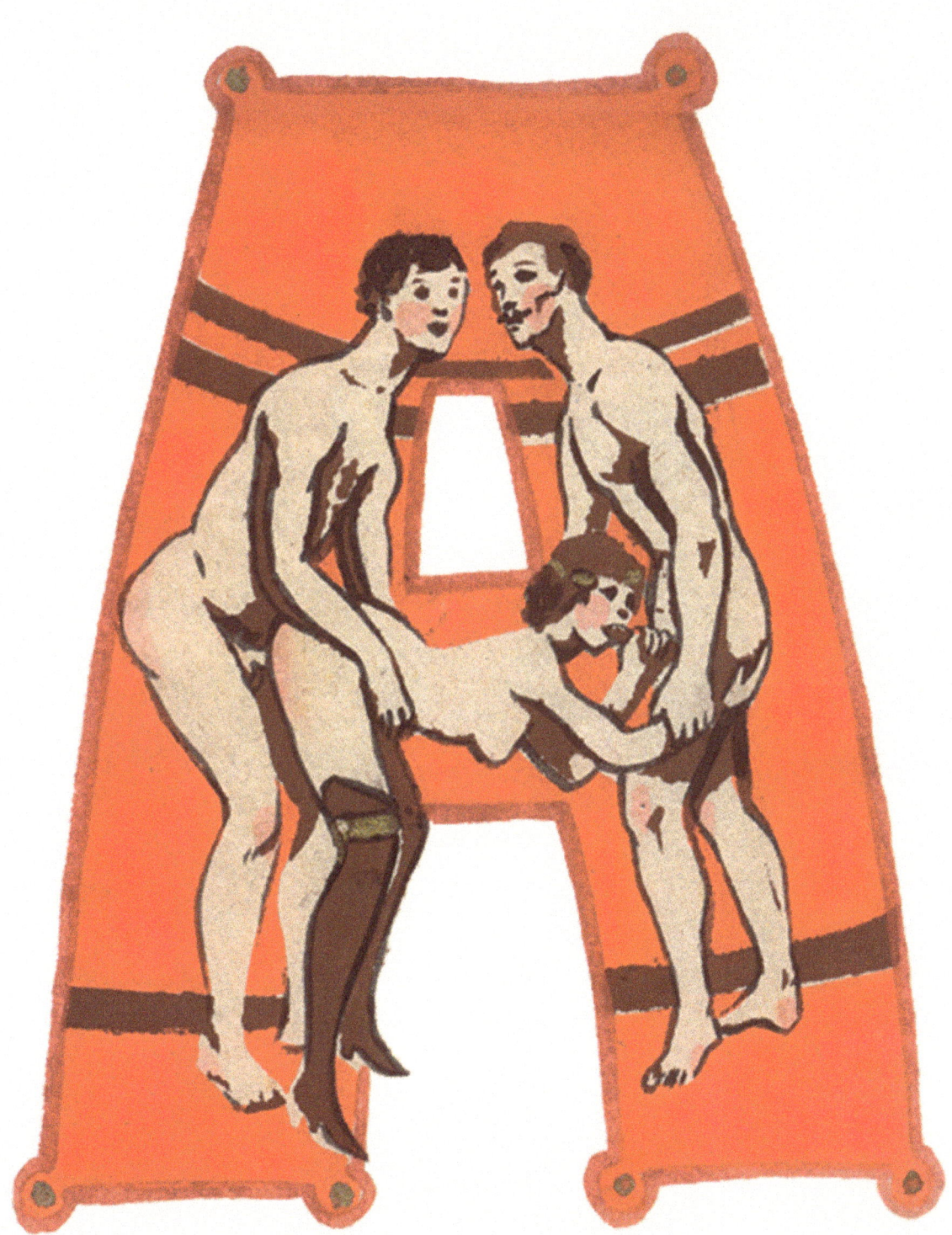

7

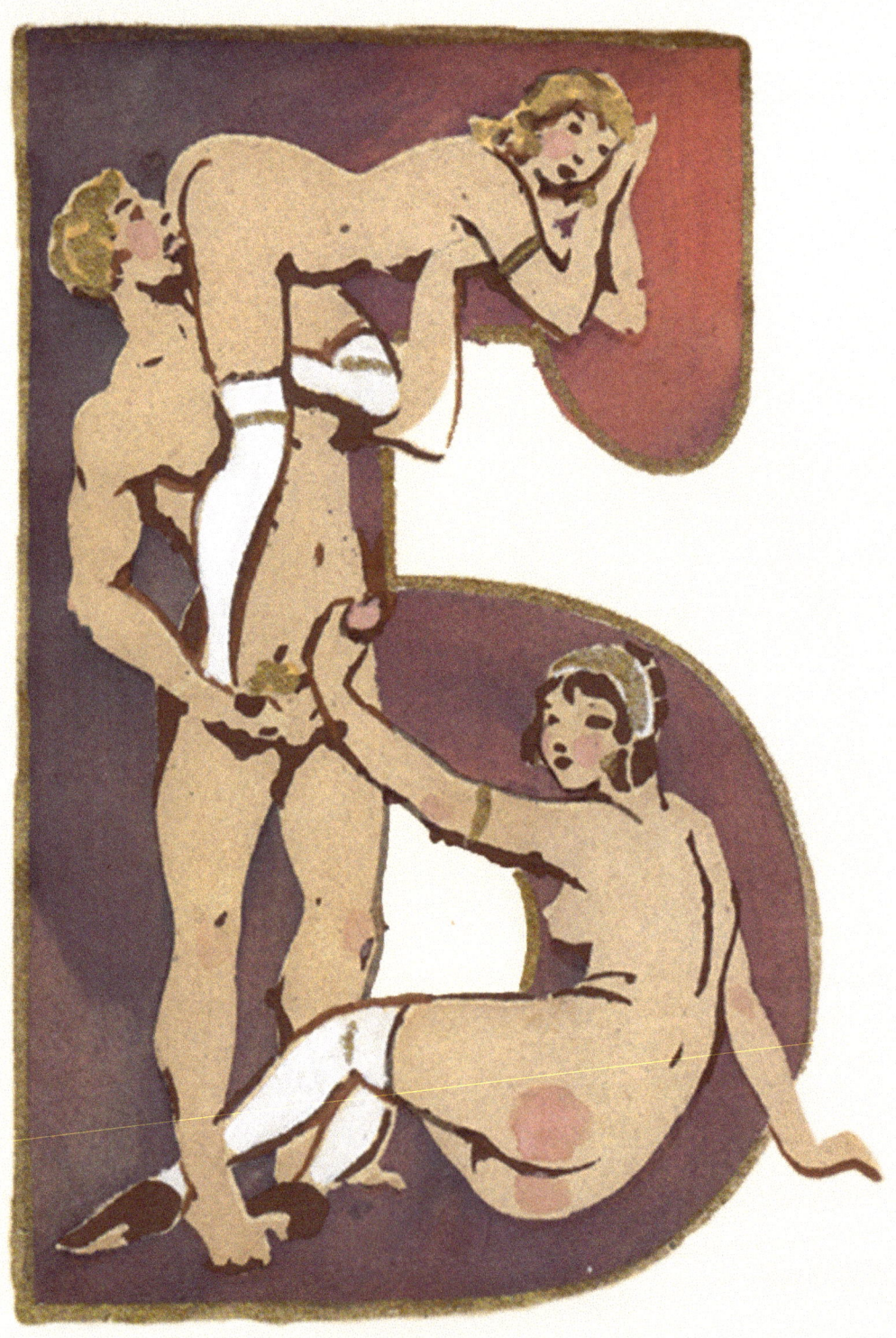

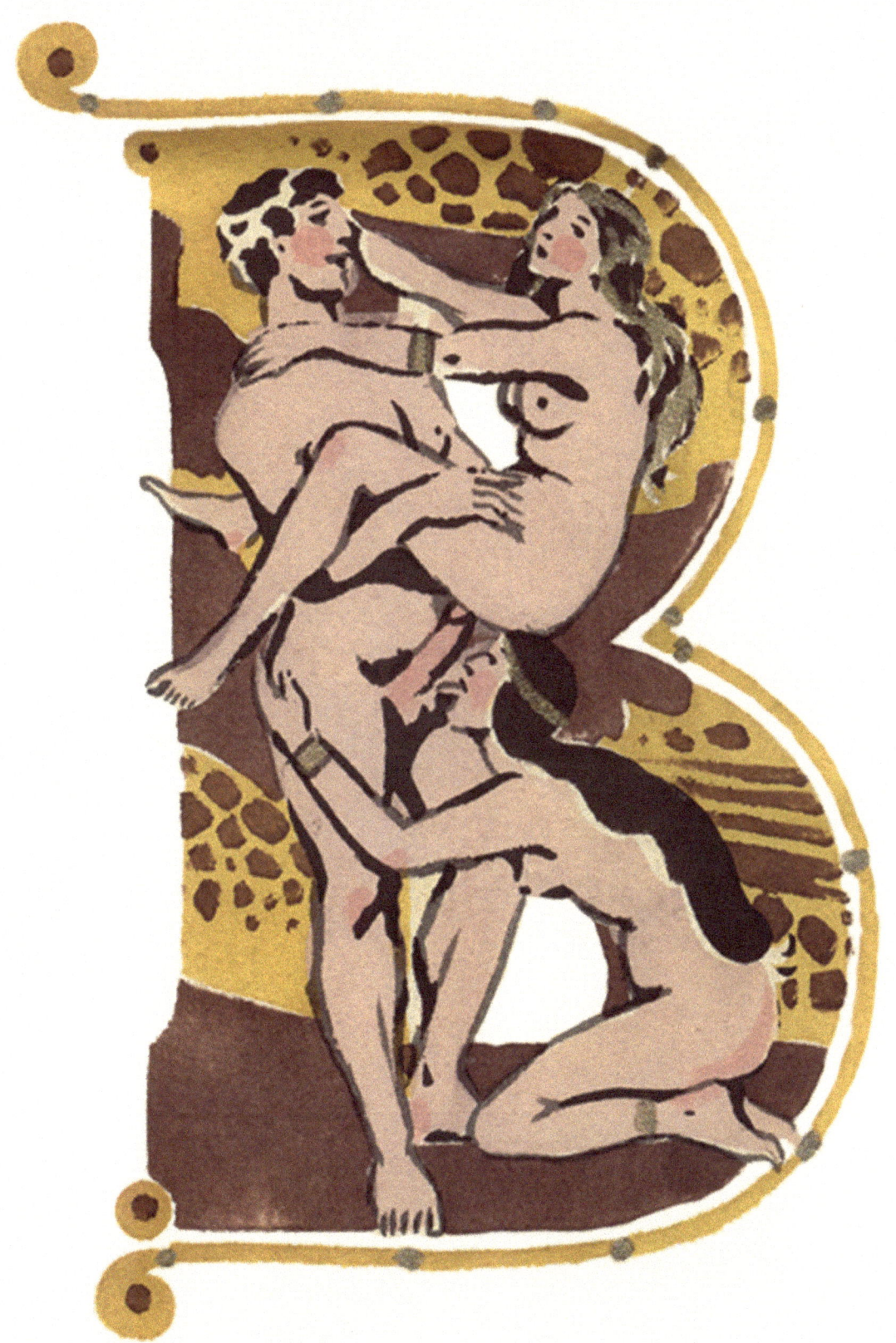

3

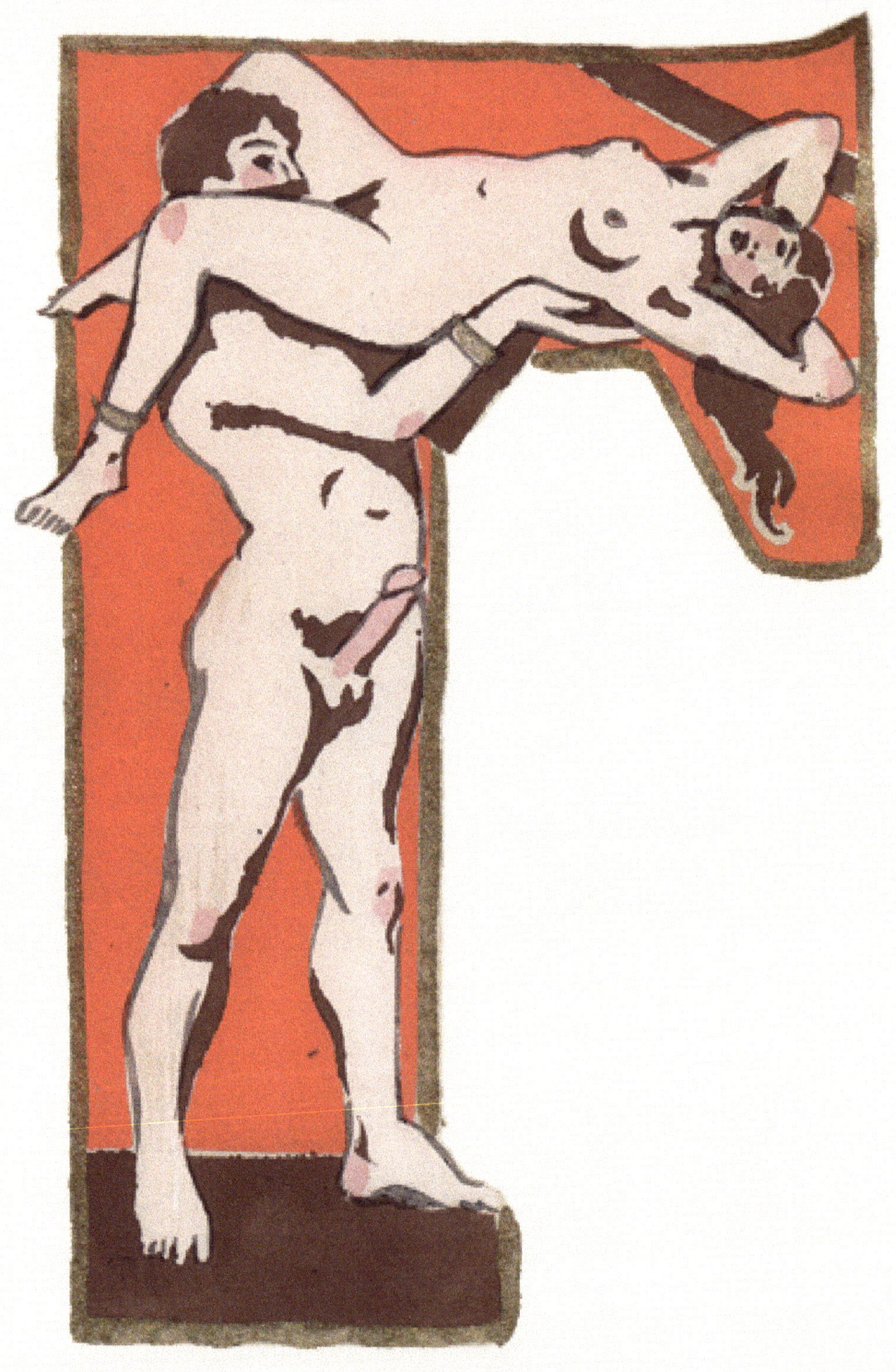

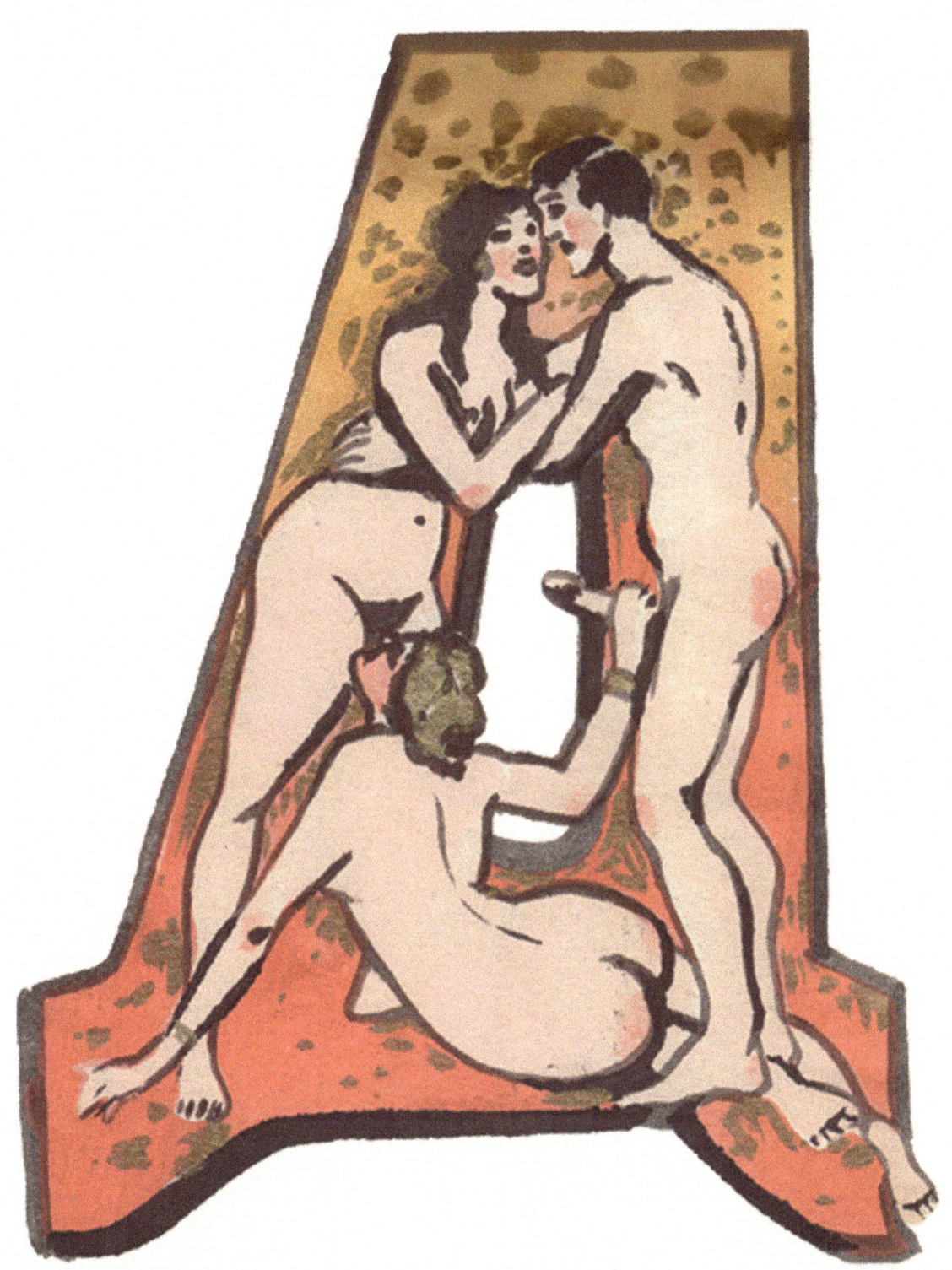

5

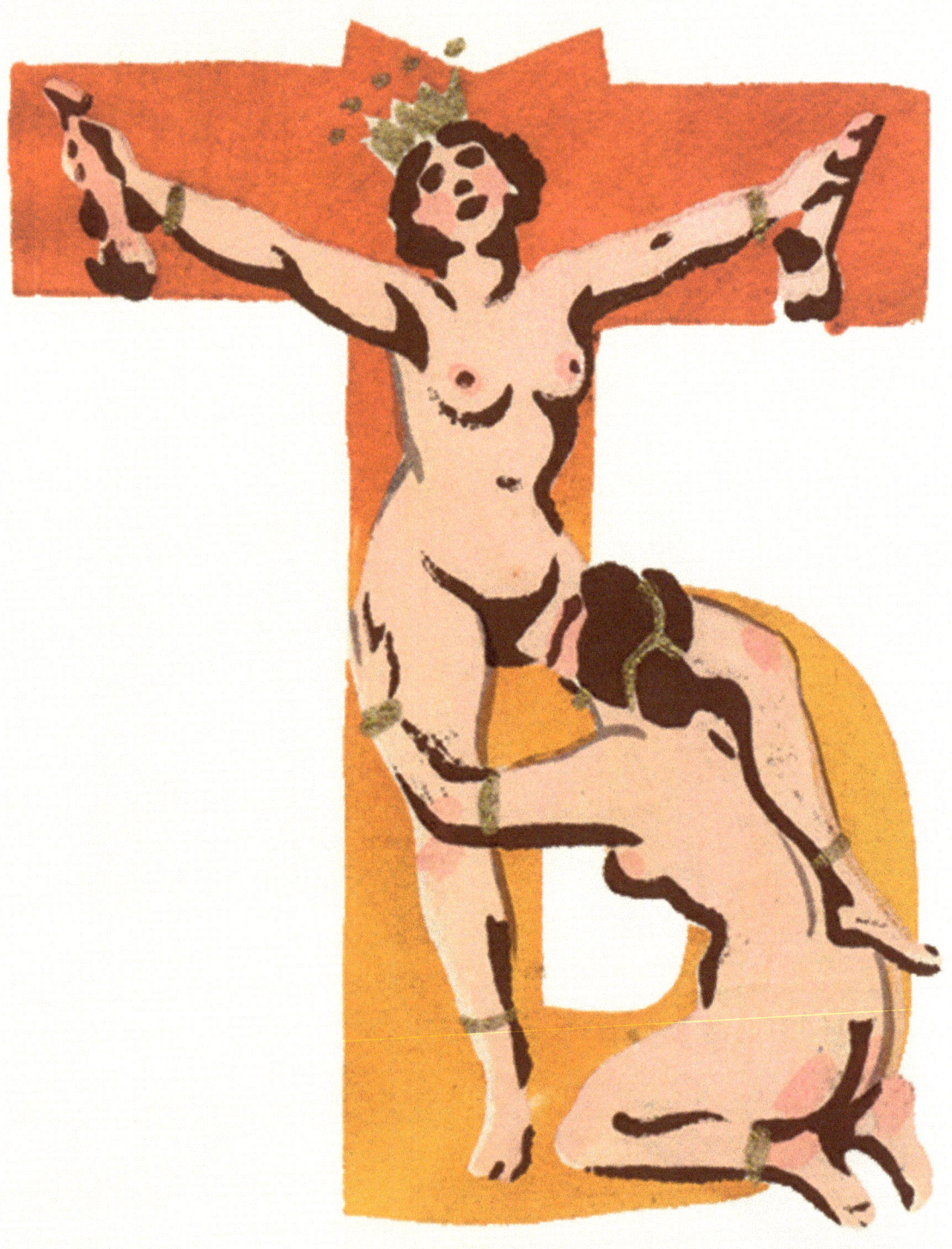

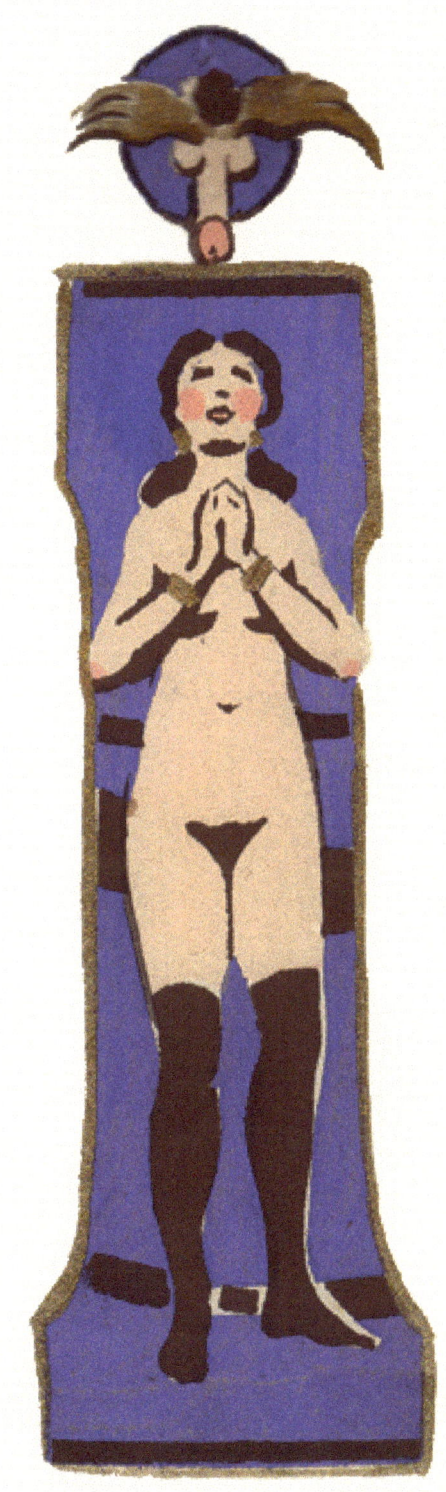

7

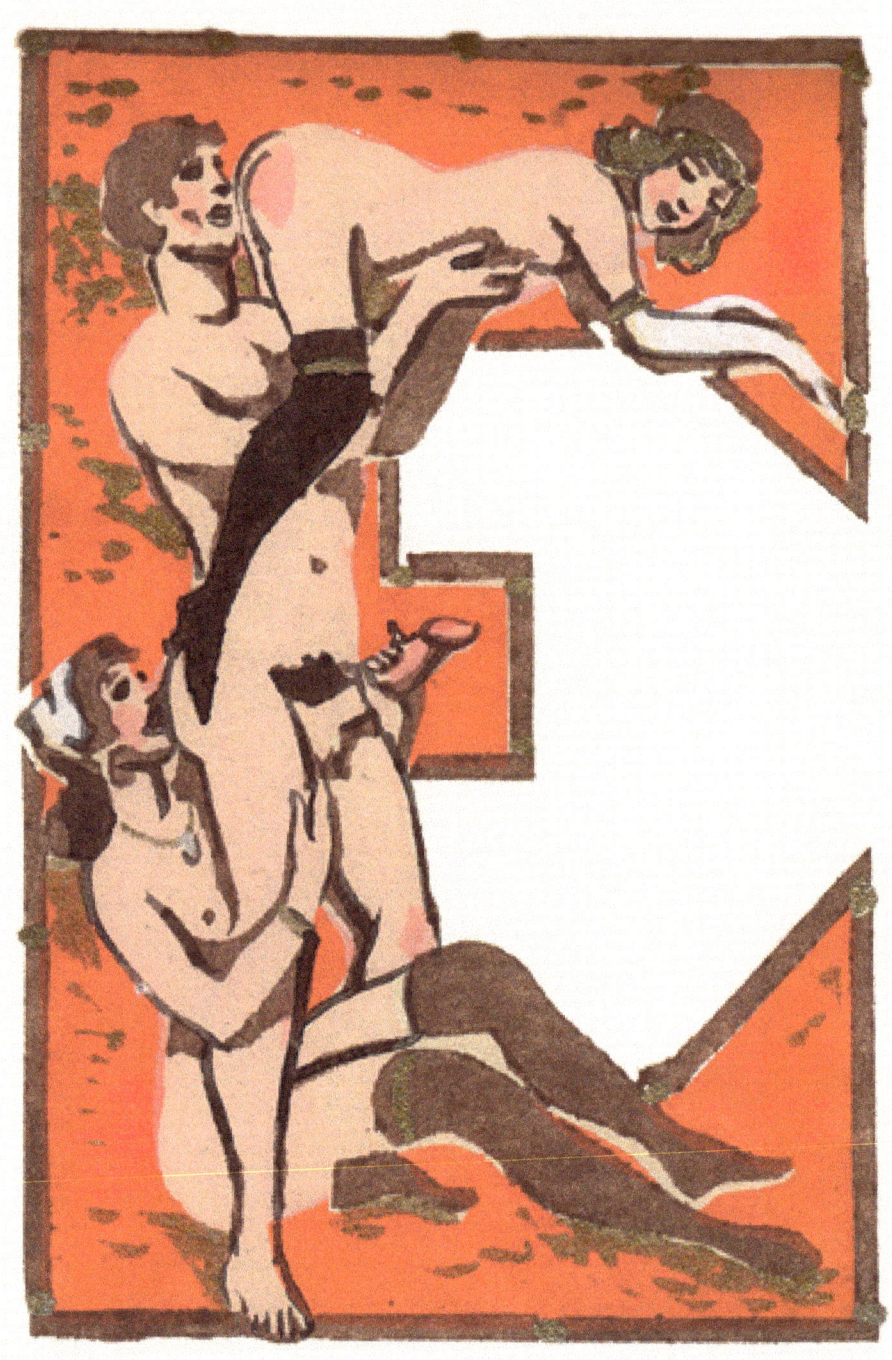

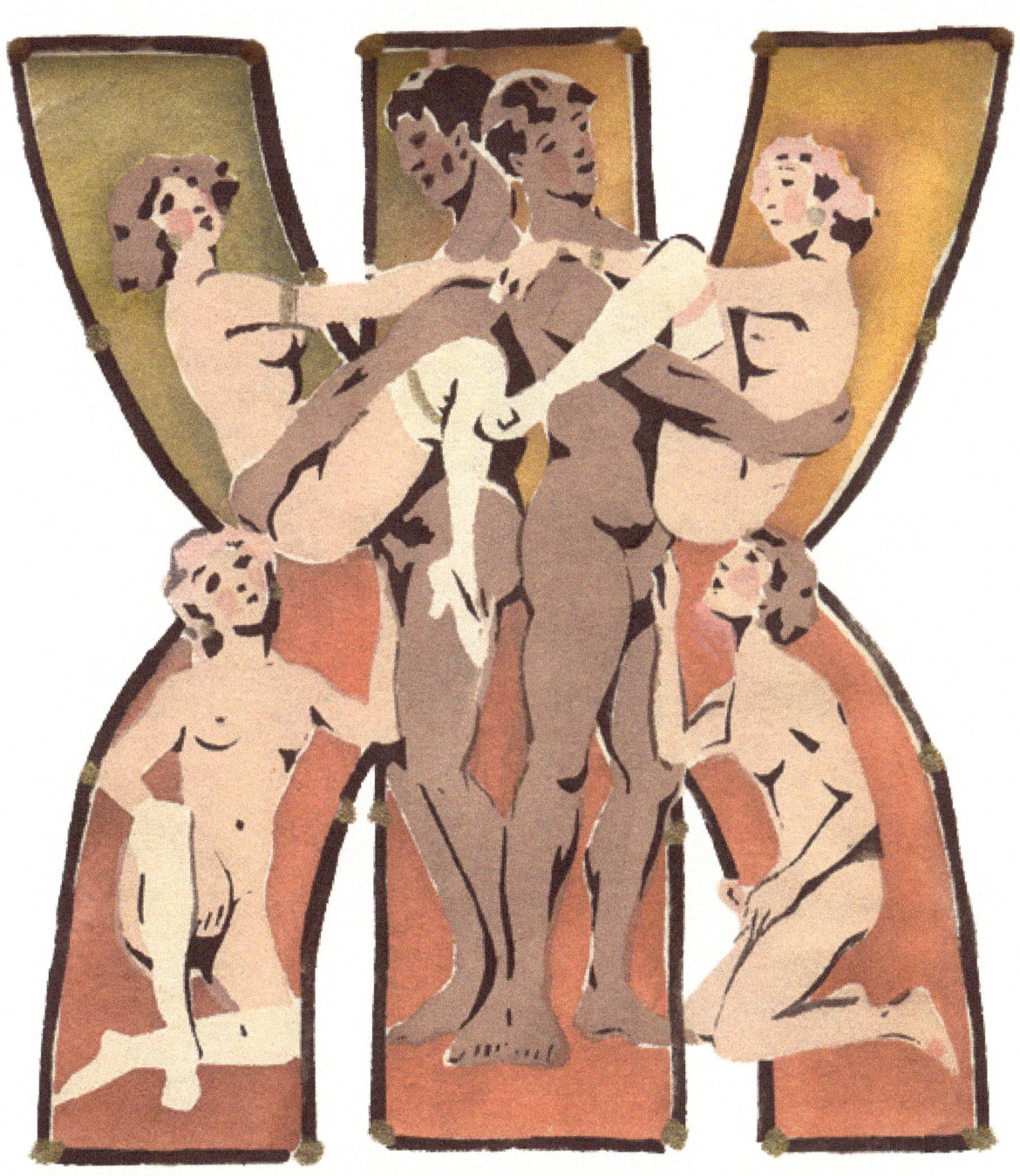

9

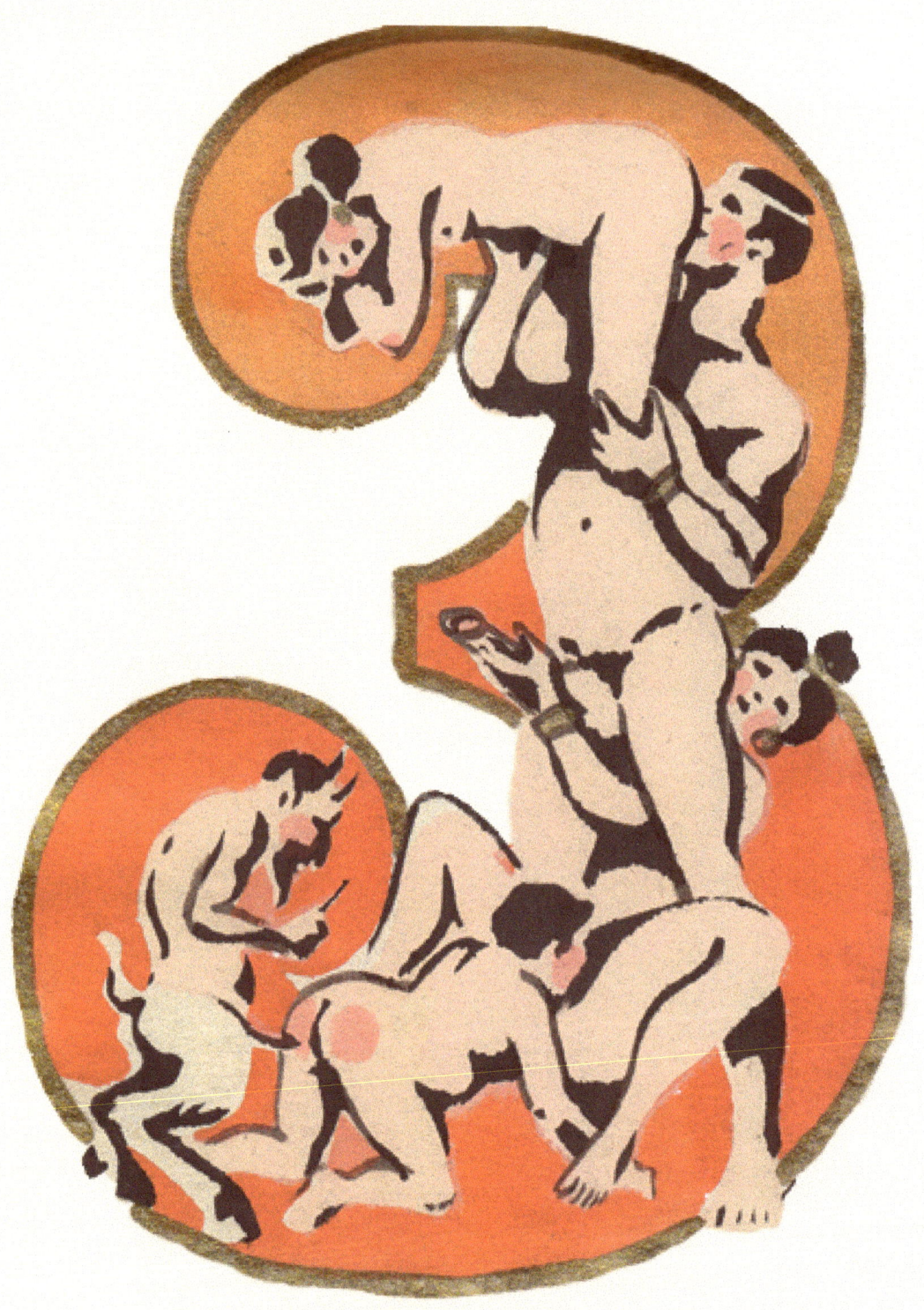

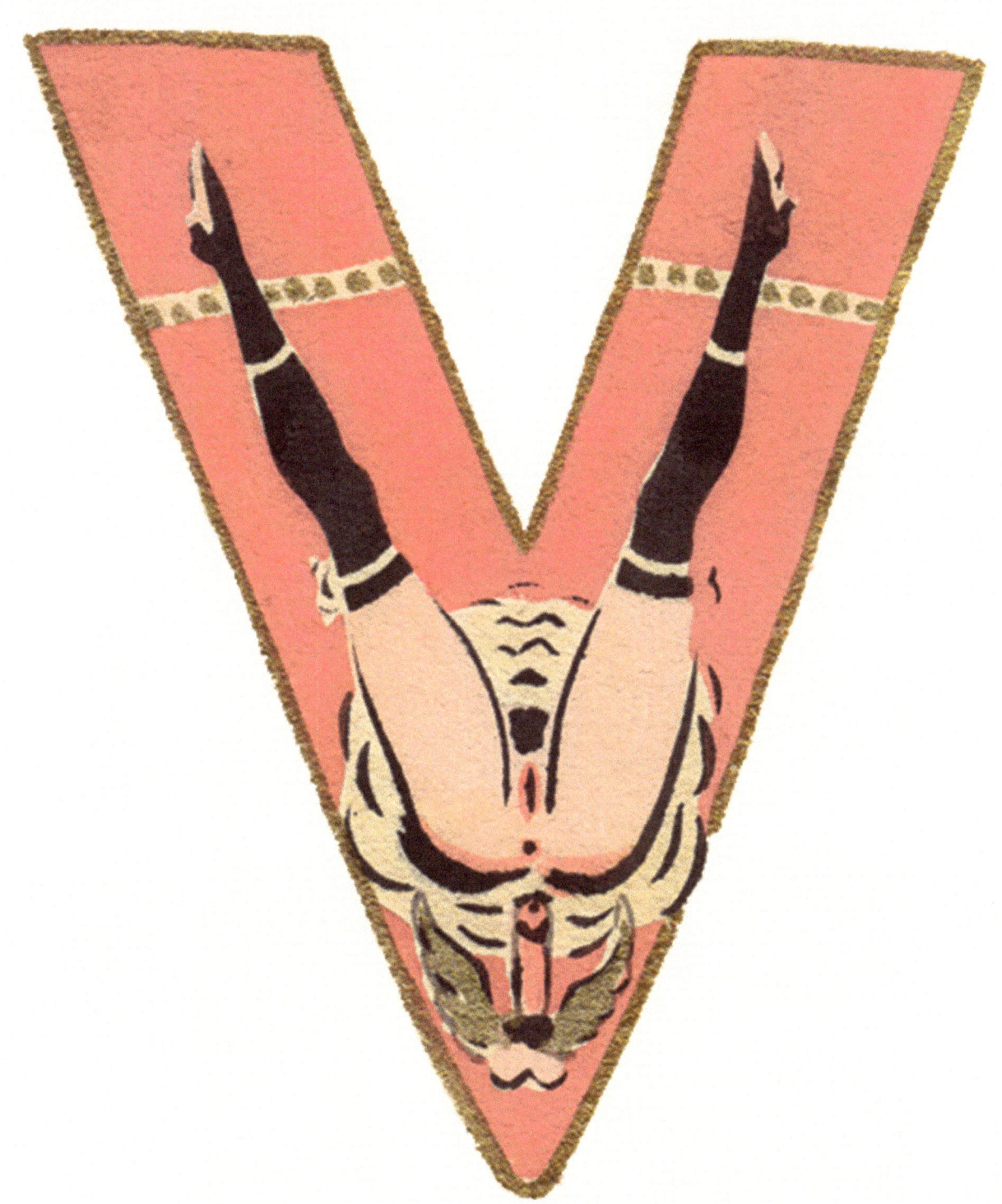

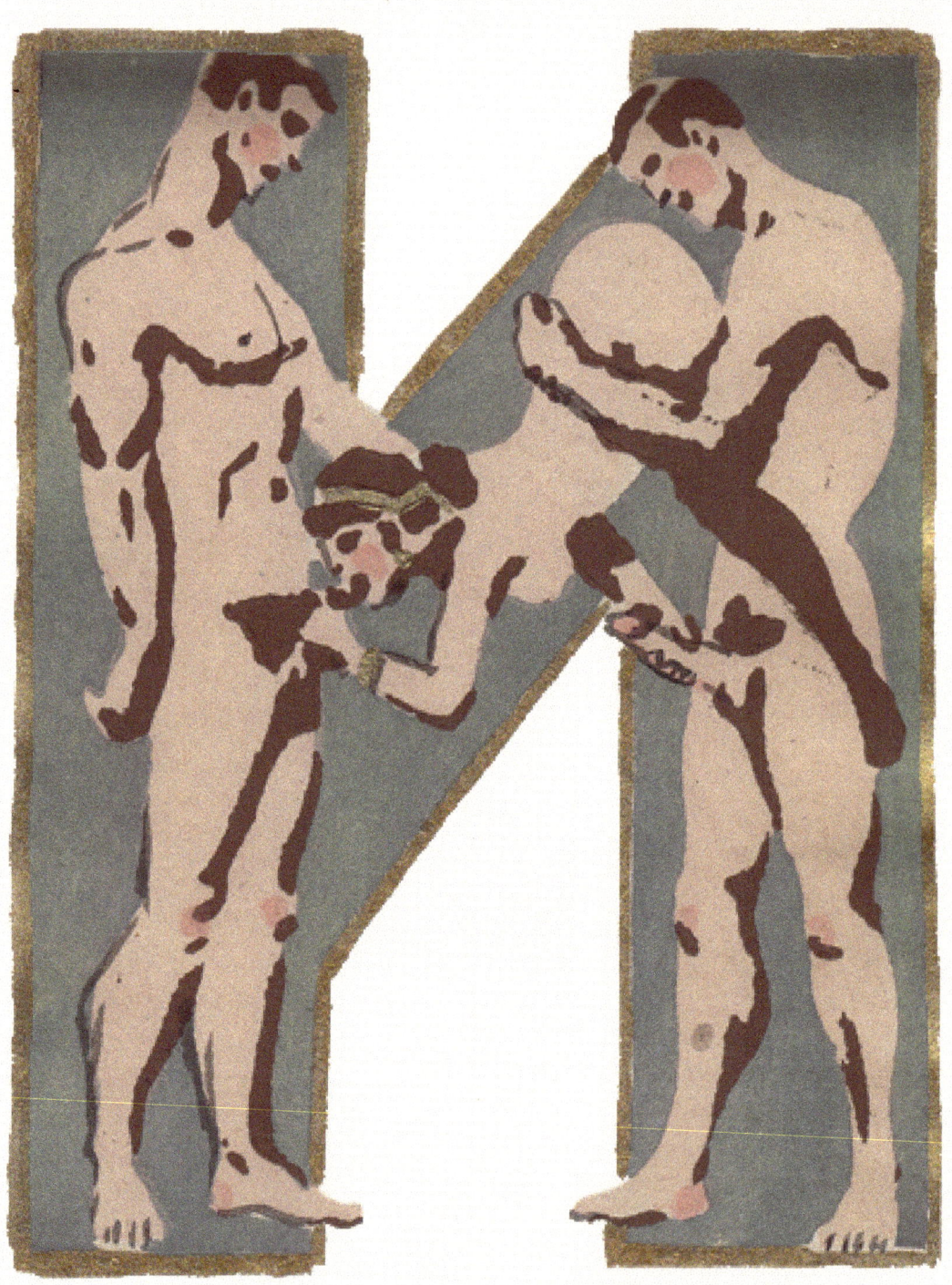

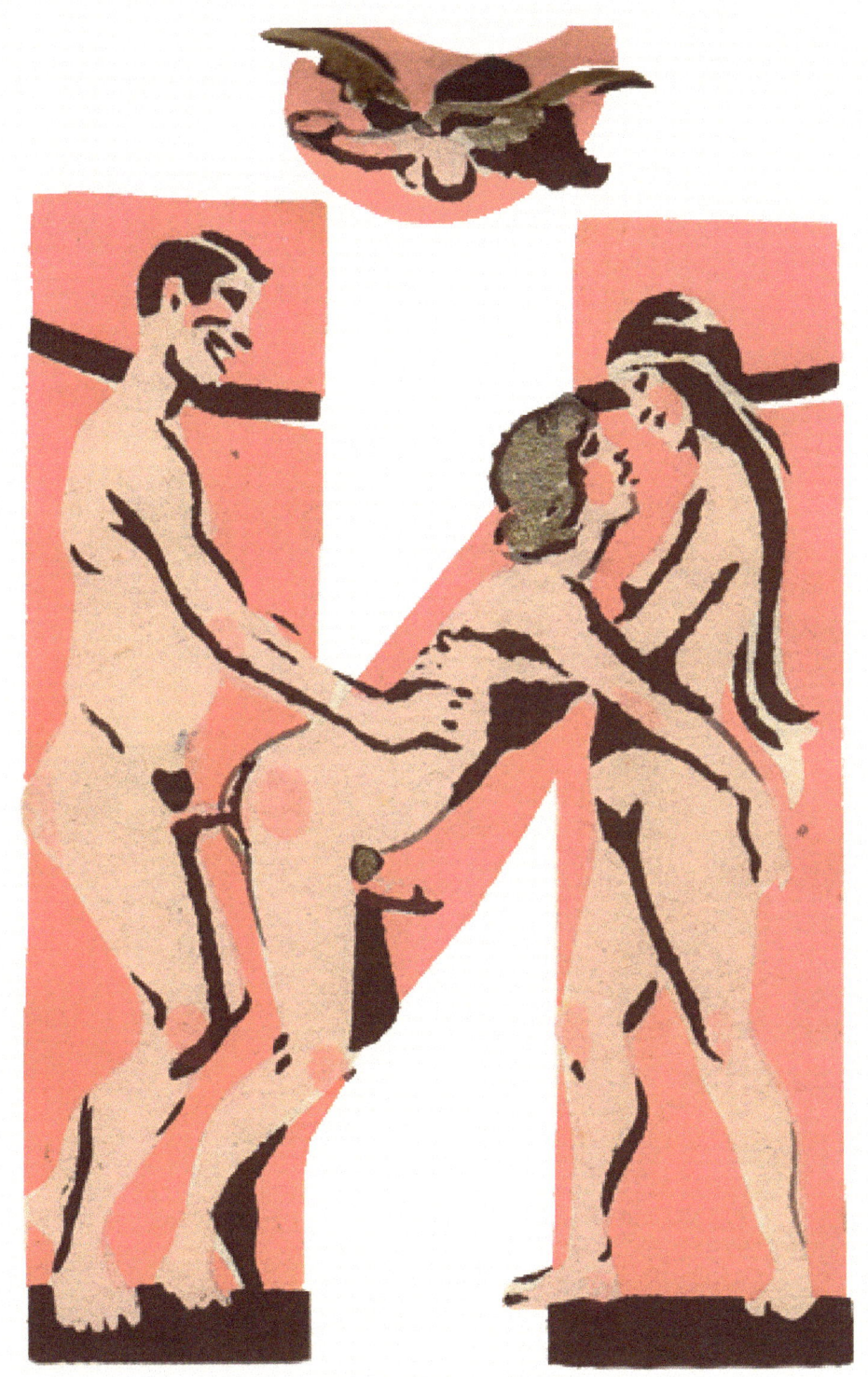

13

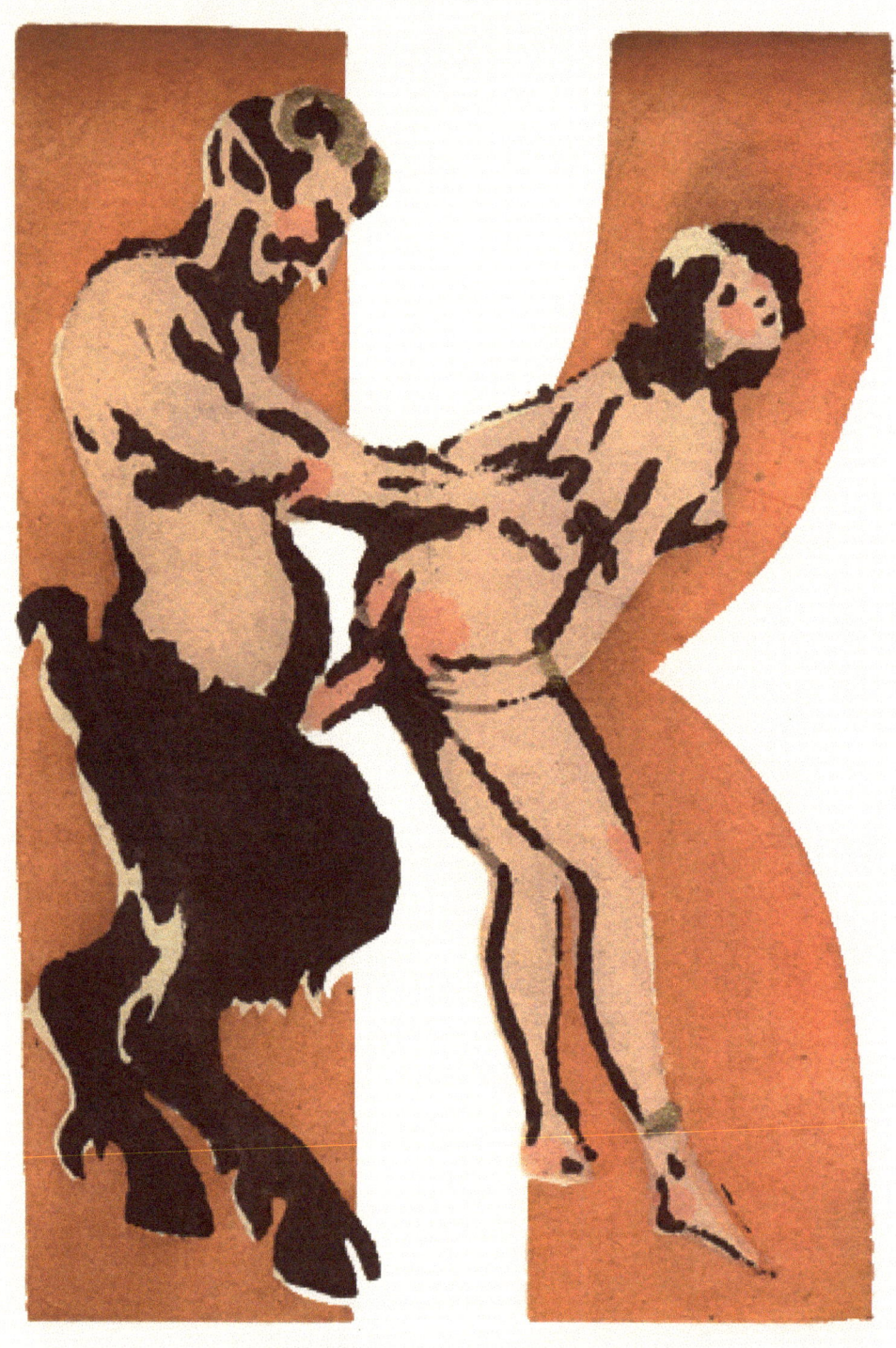

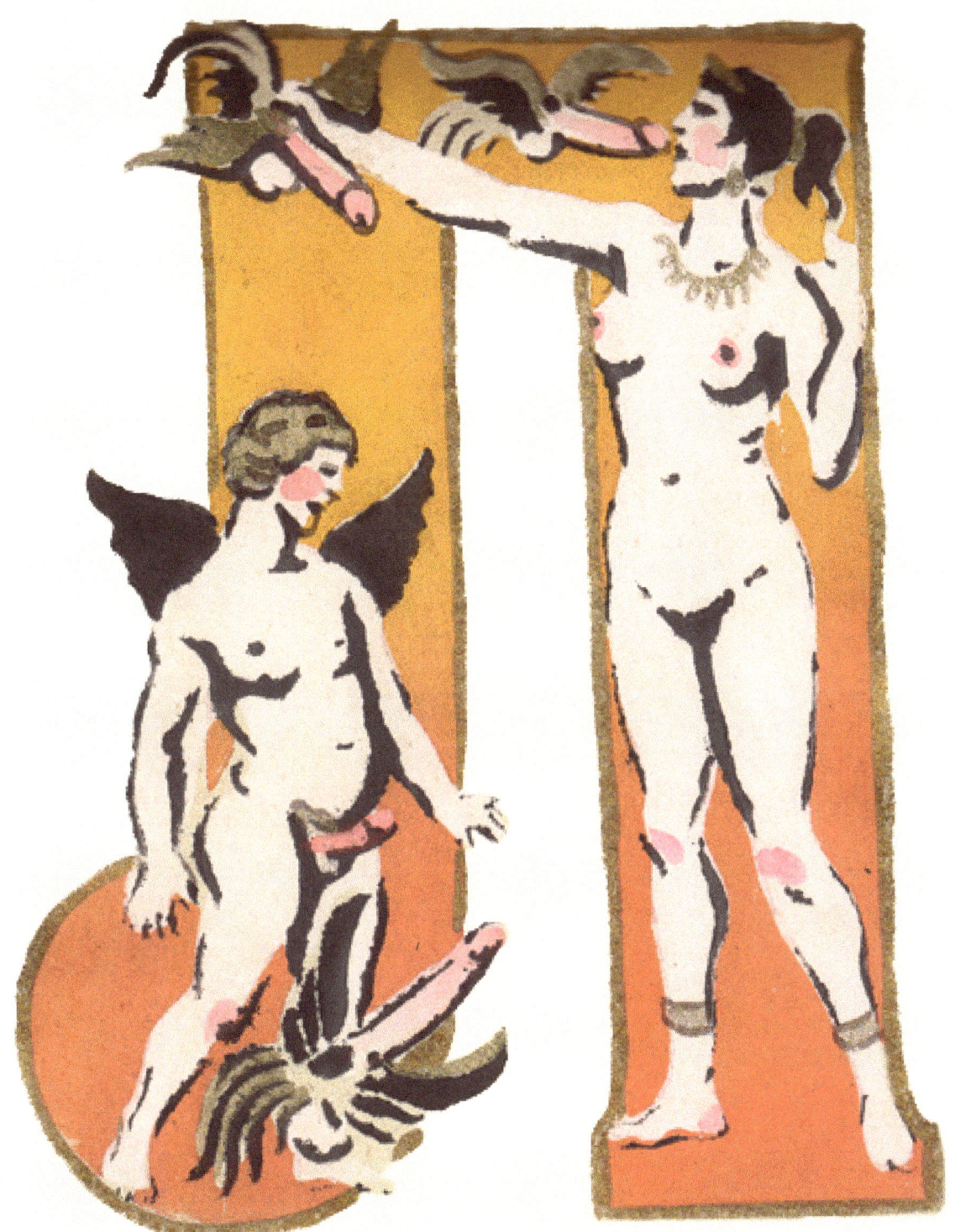

15

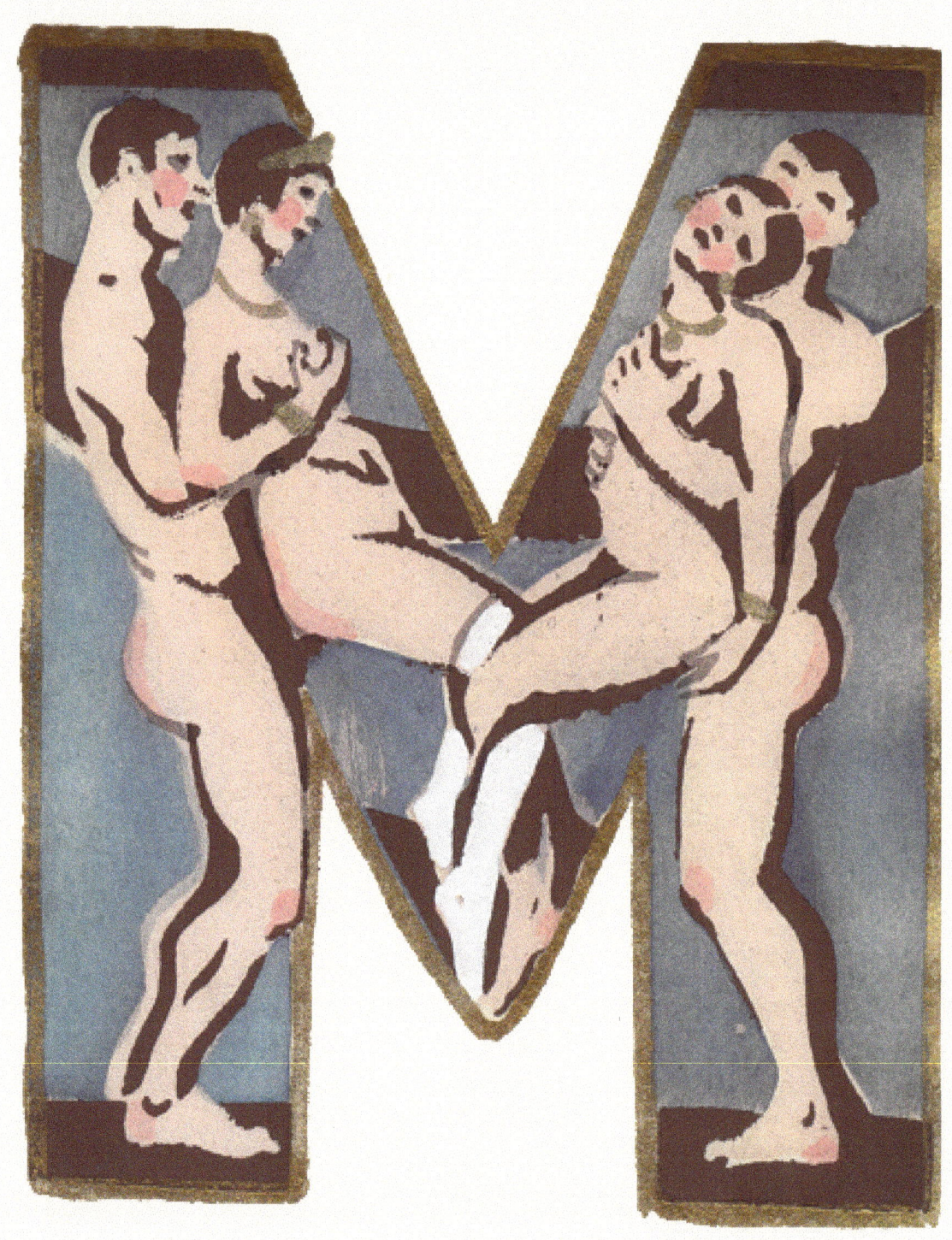

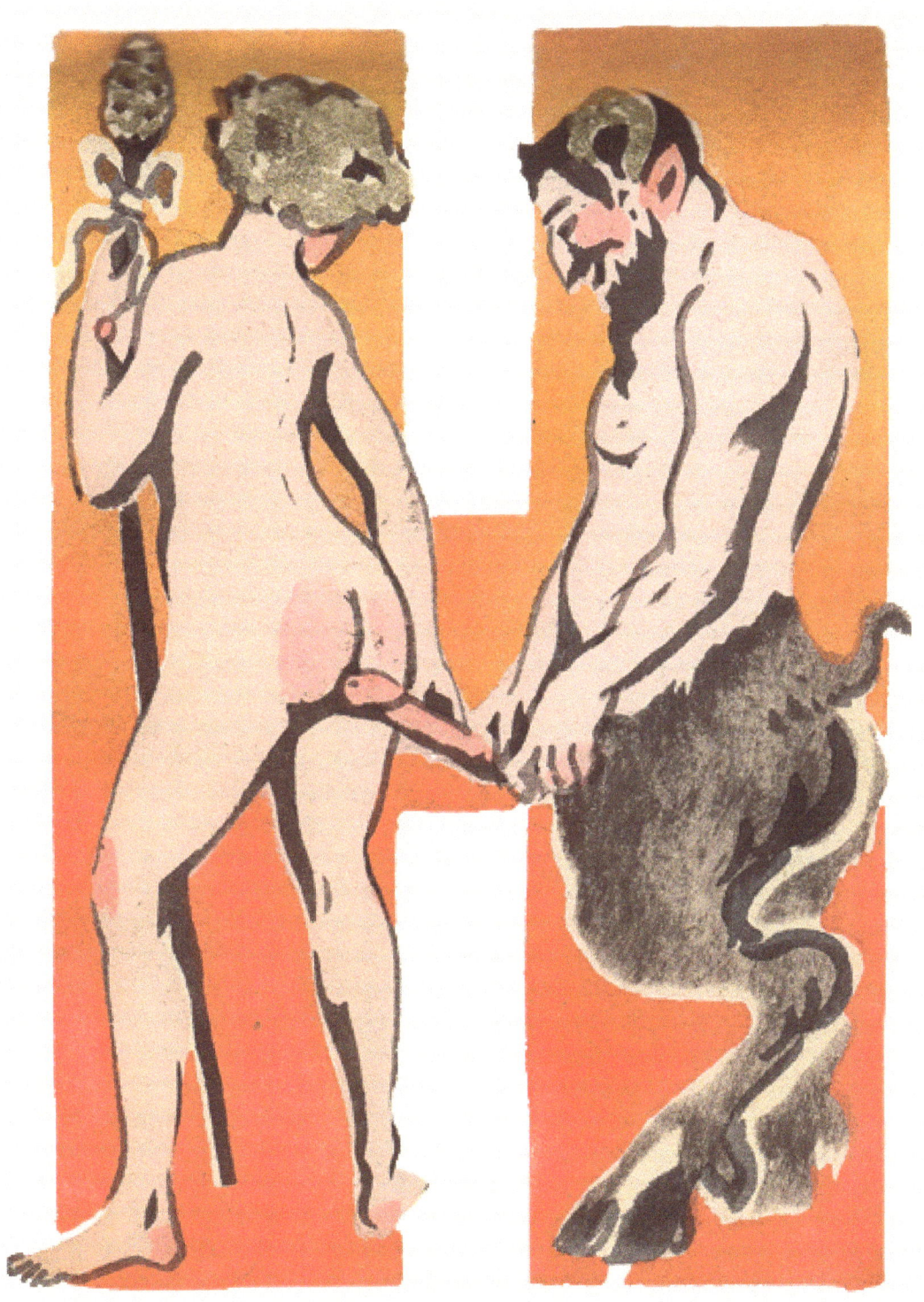

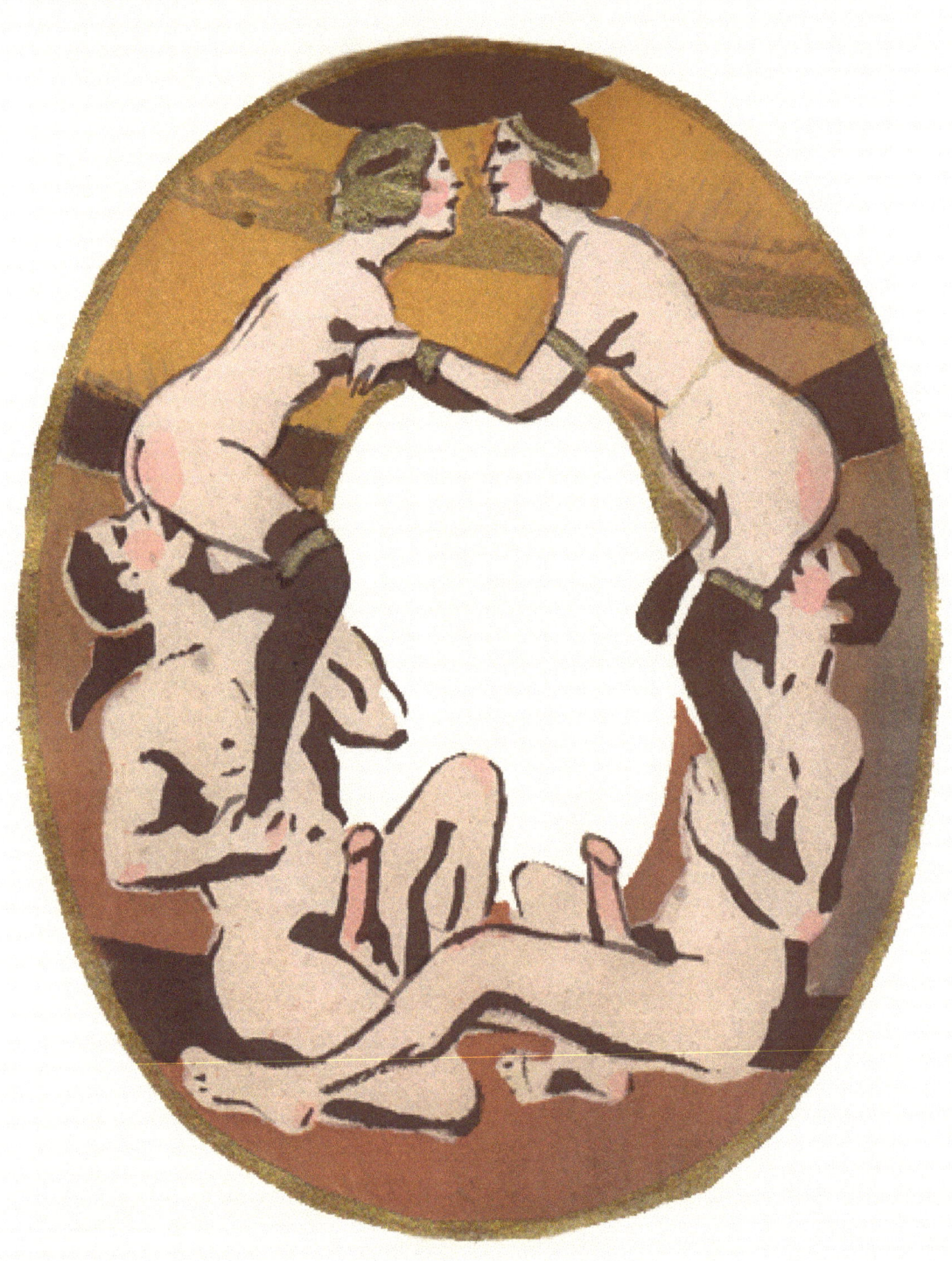

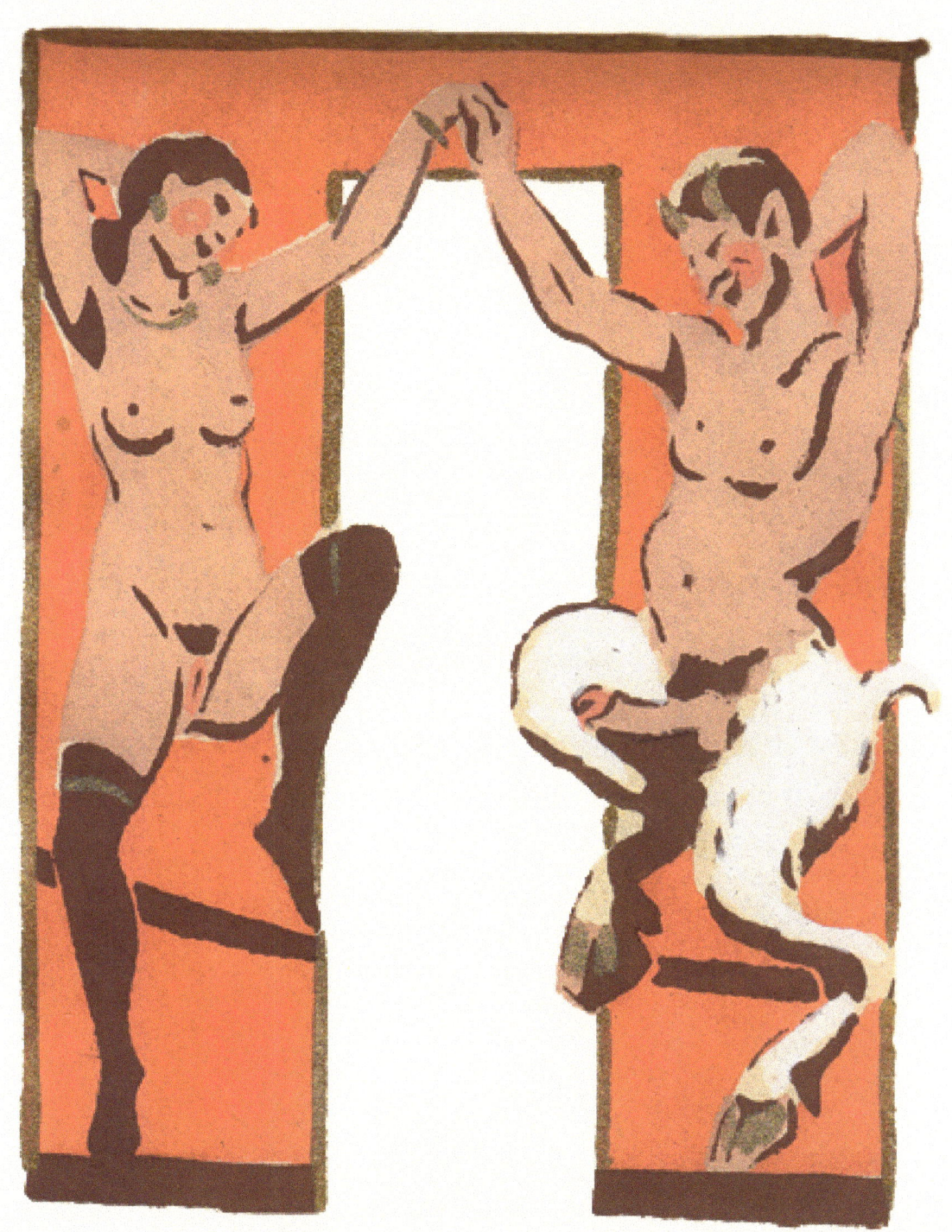

19

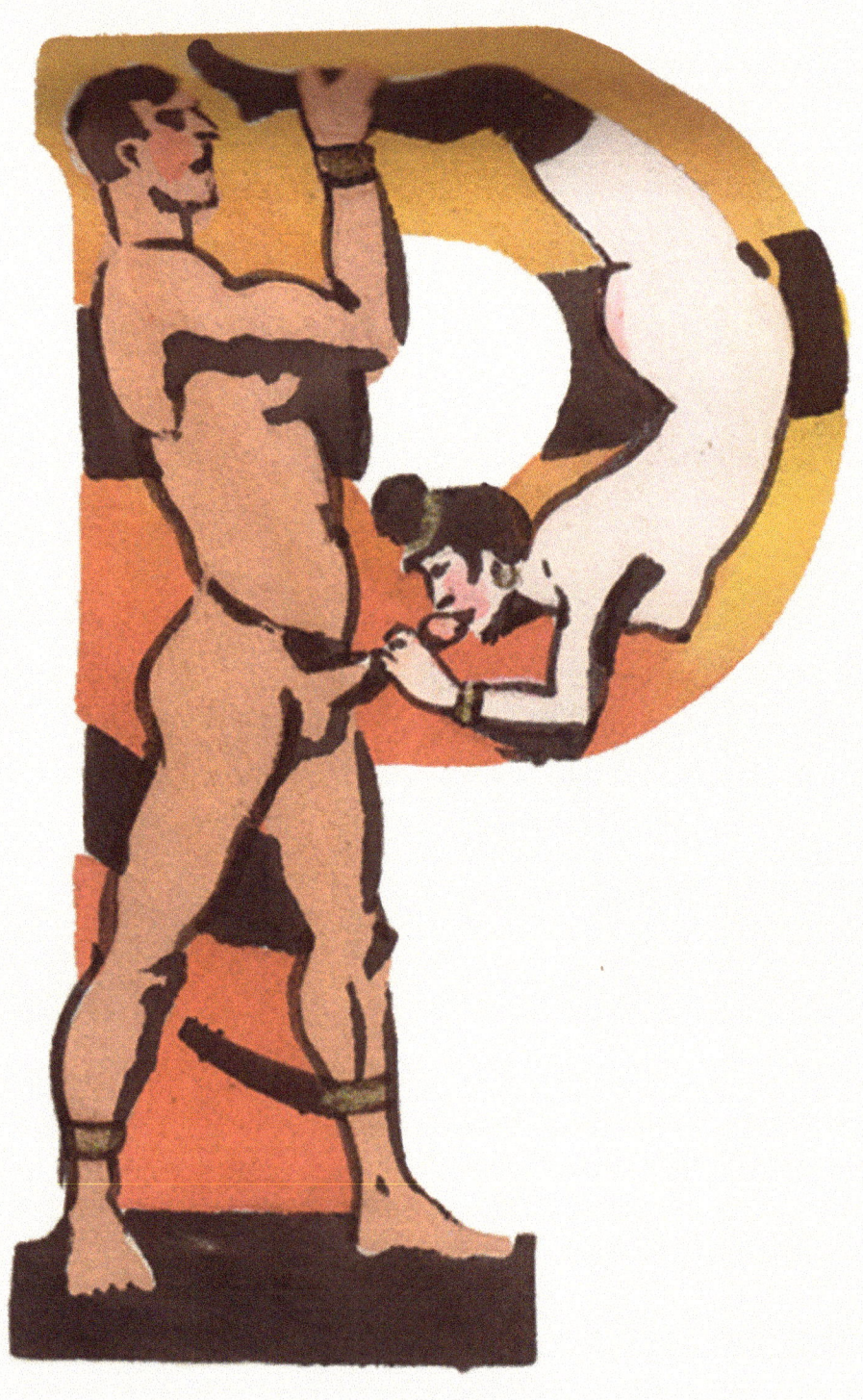

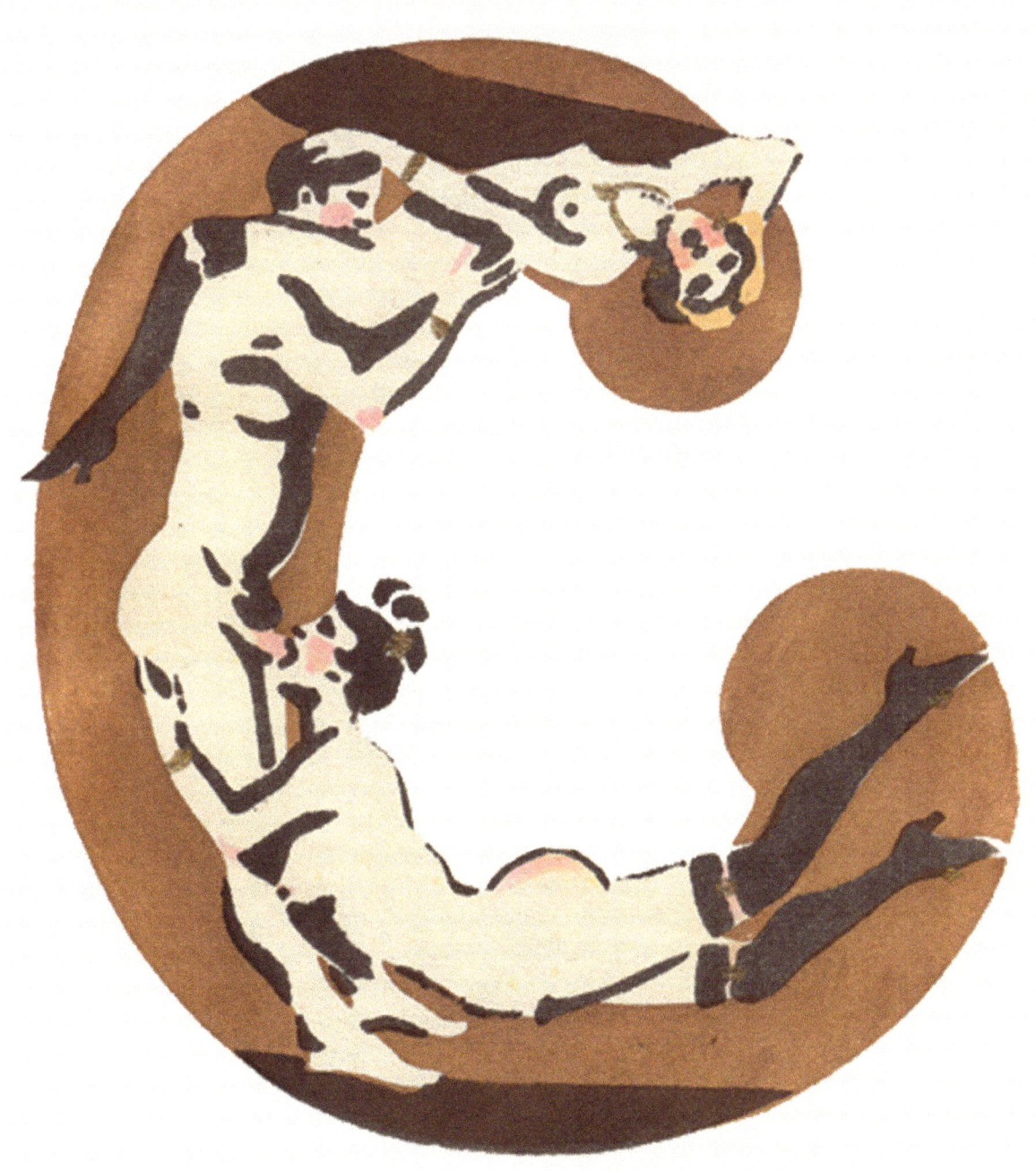

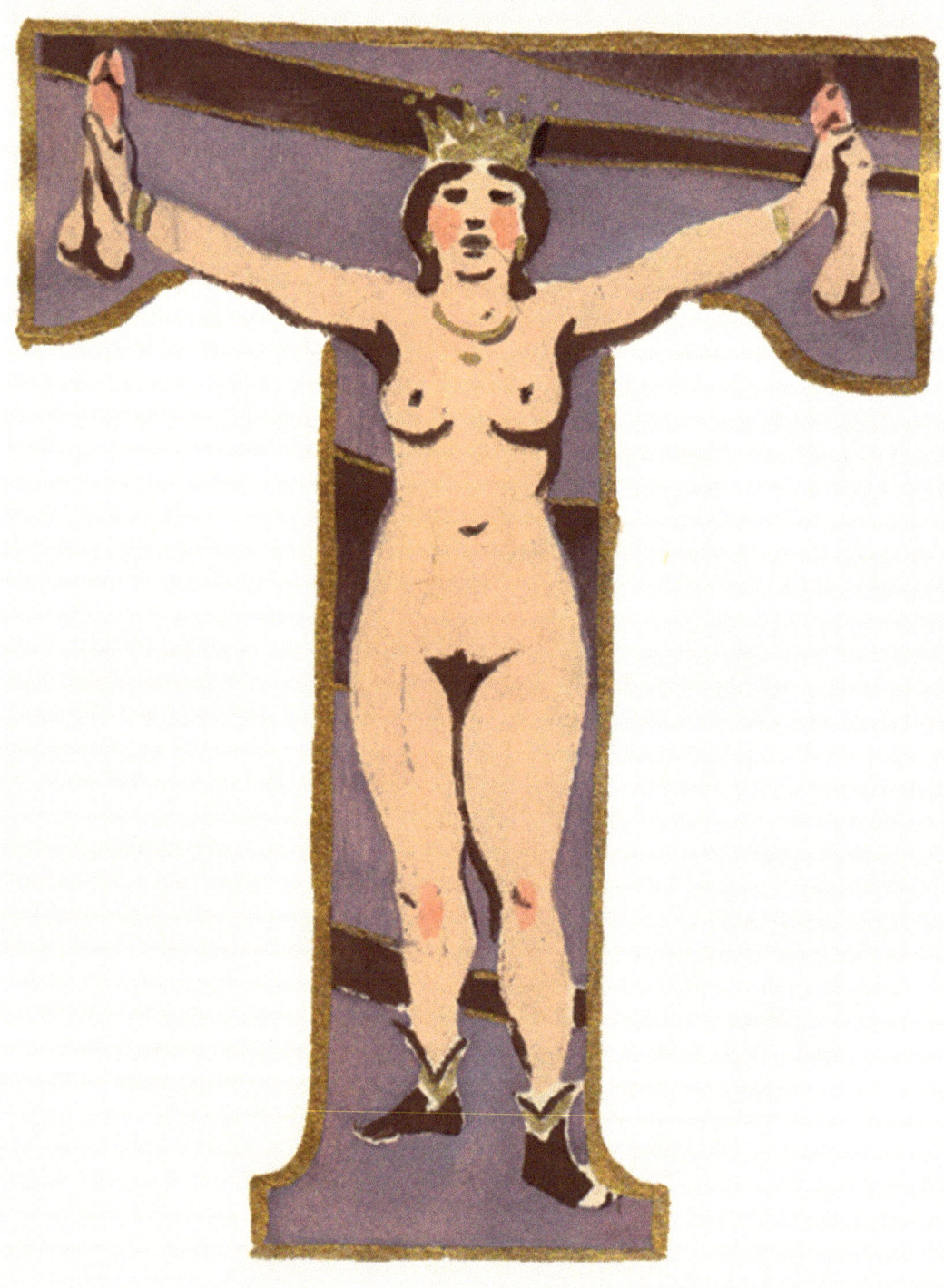

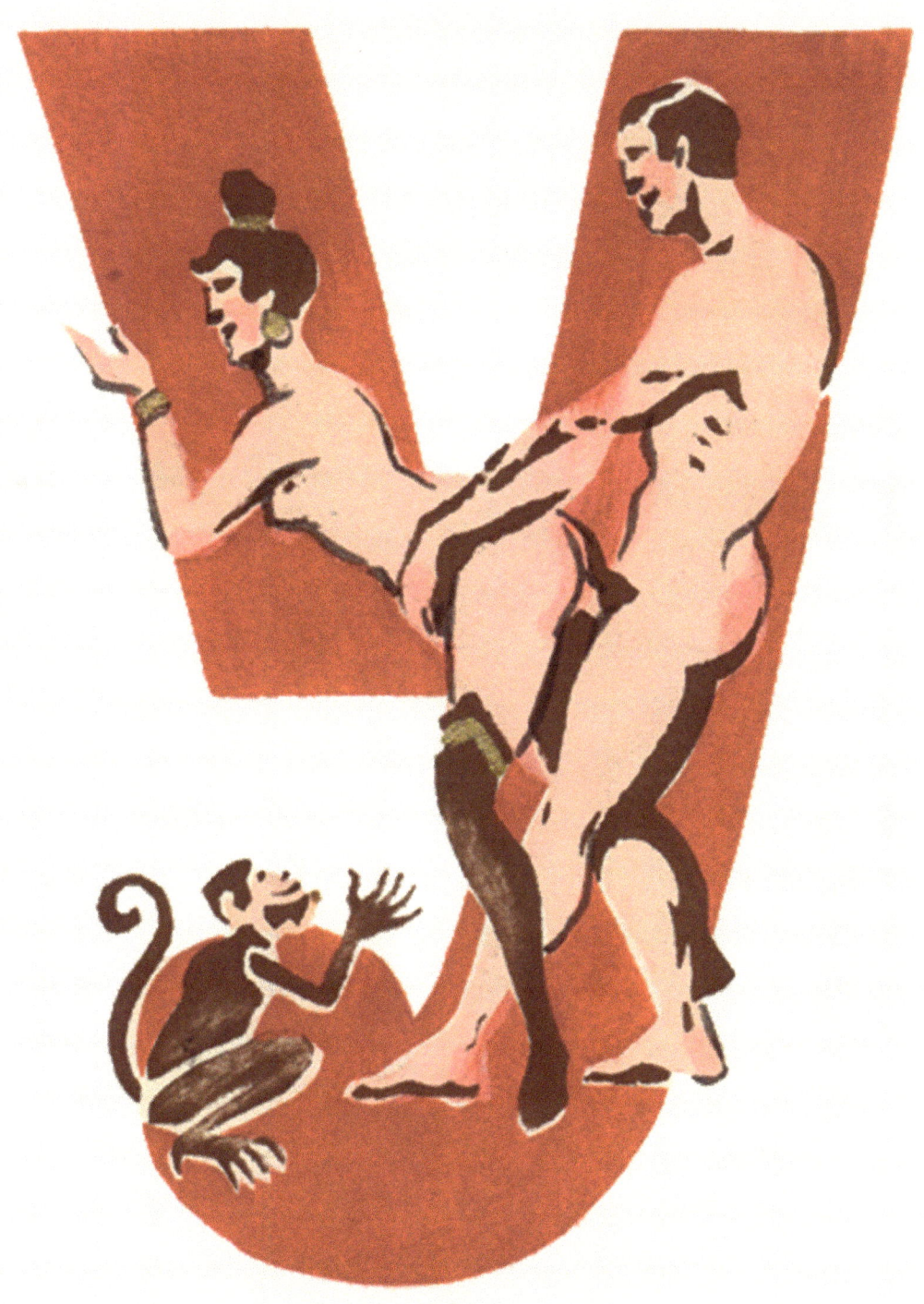

23

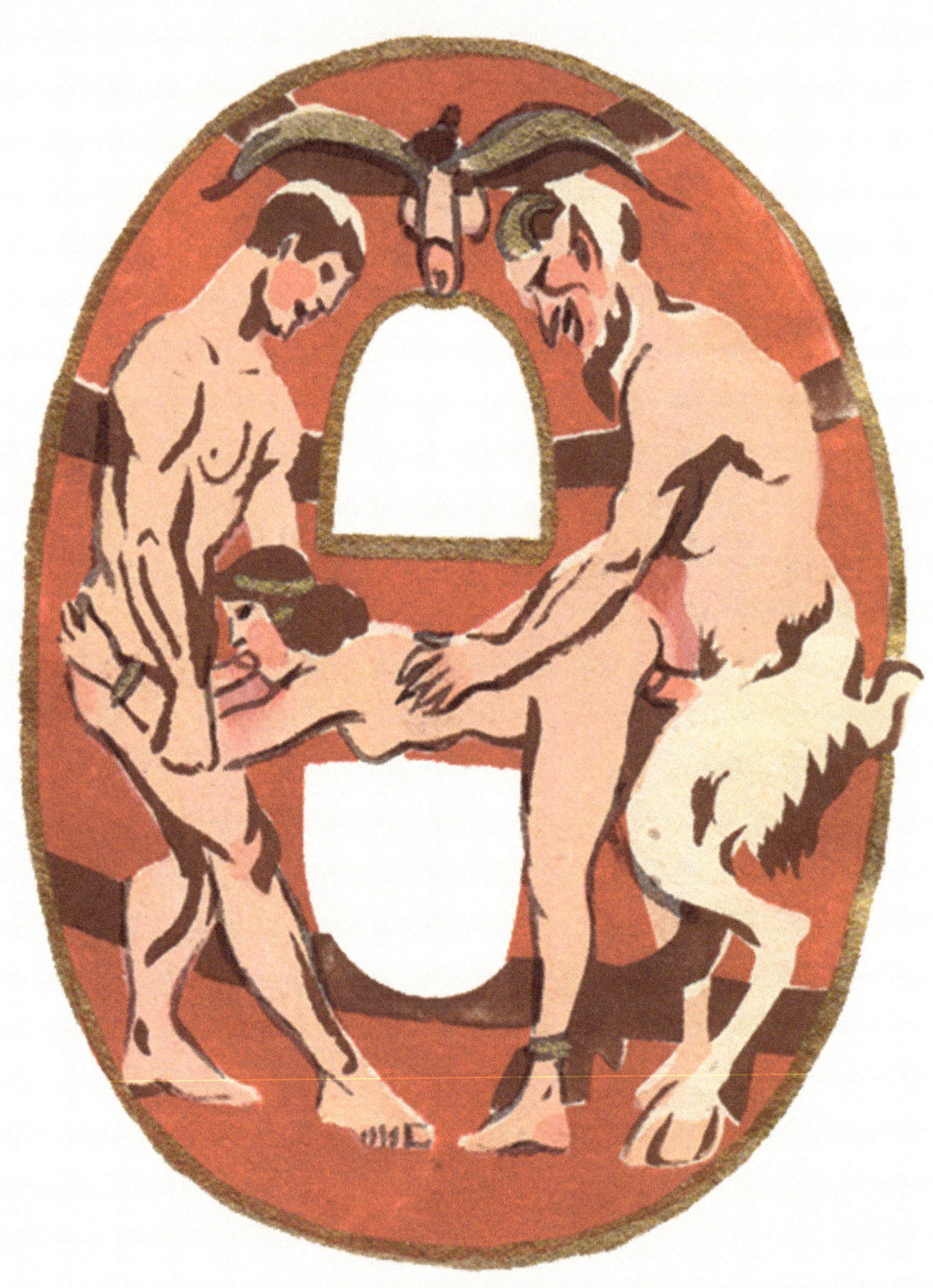

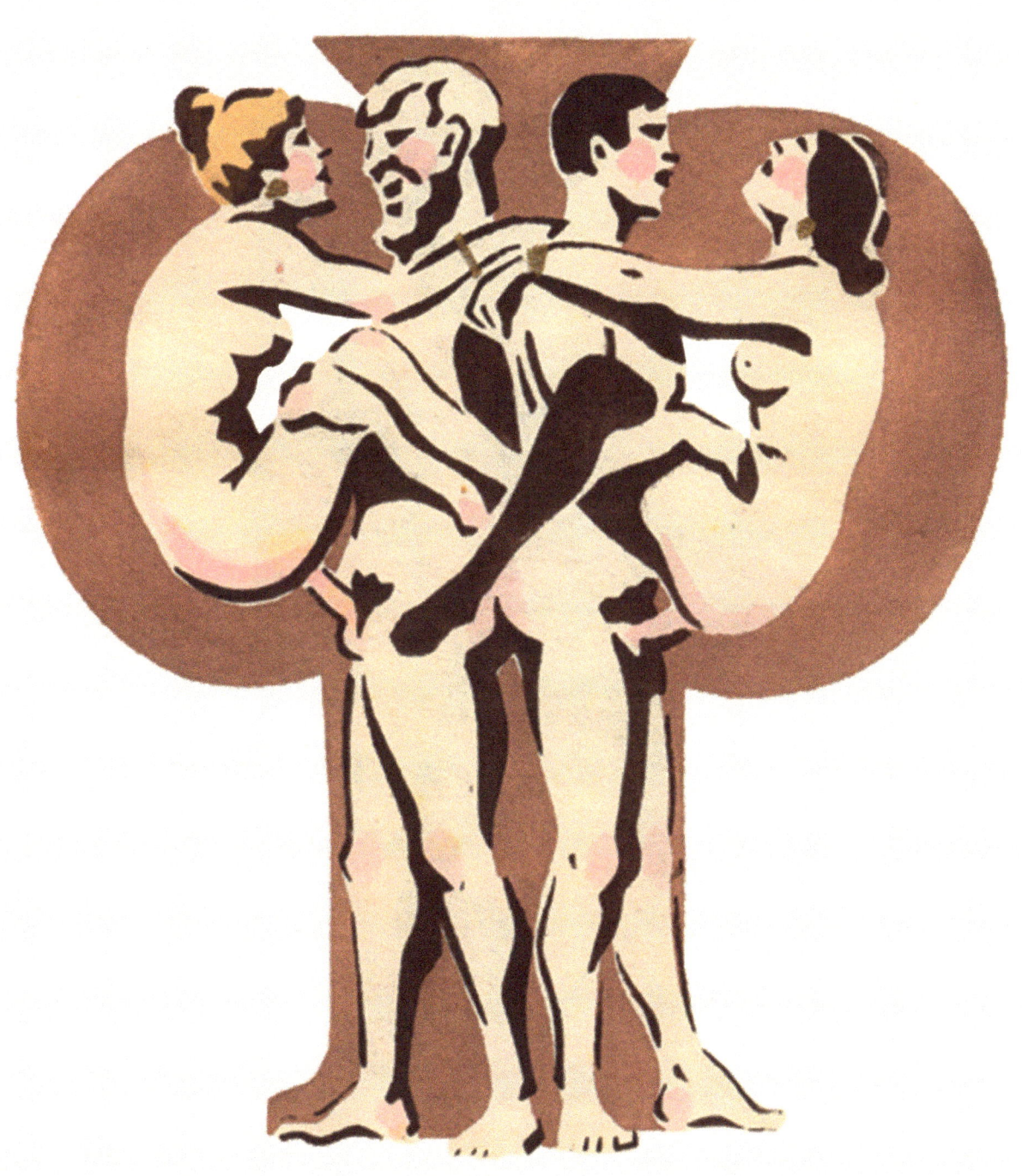

25

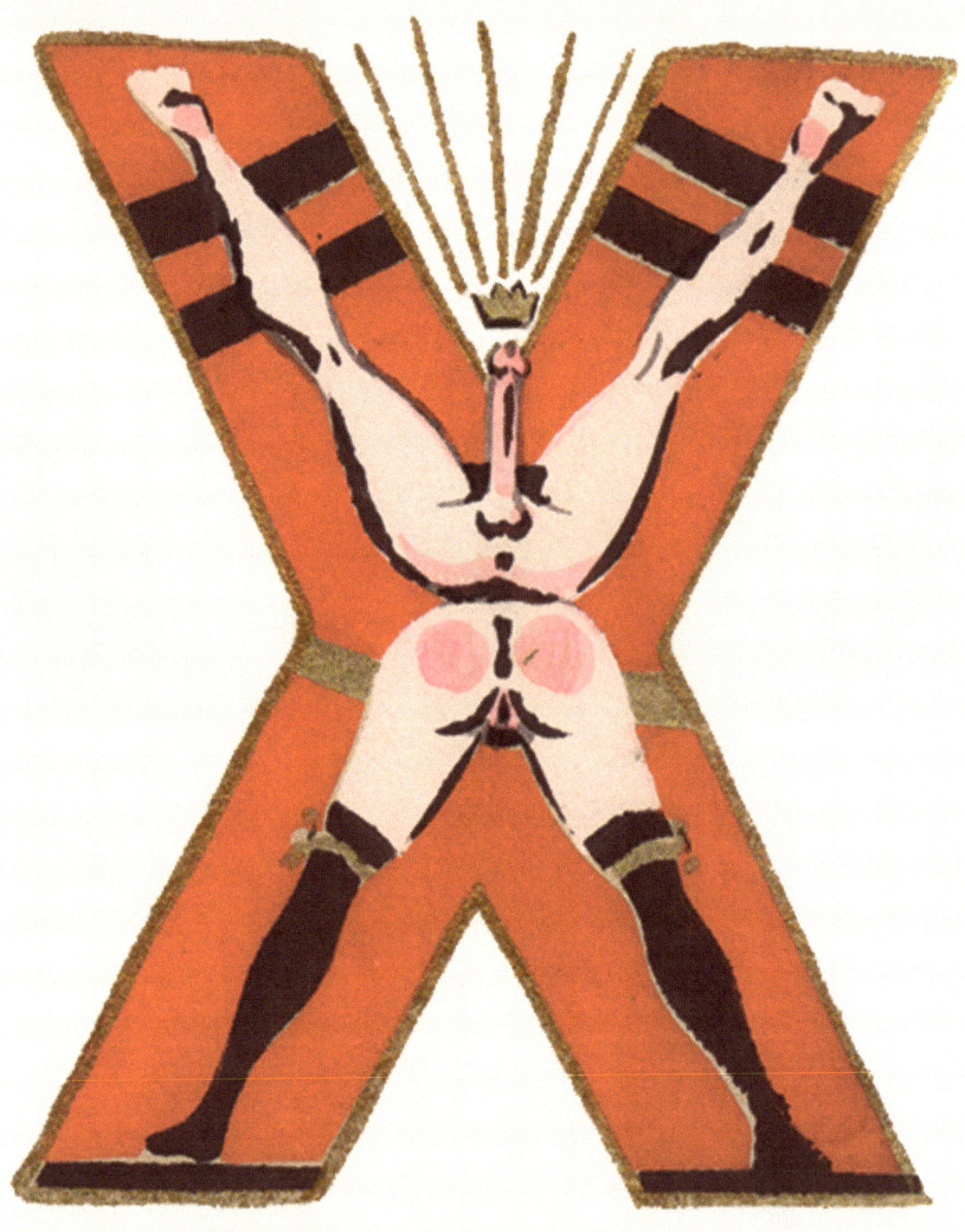

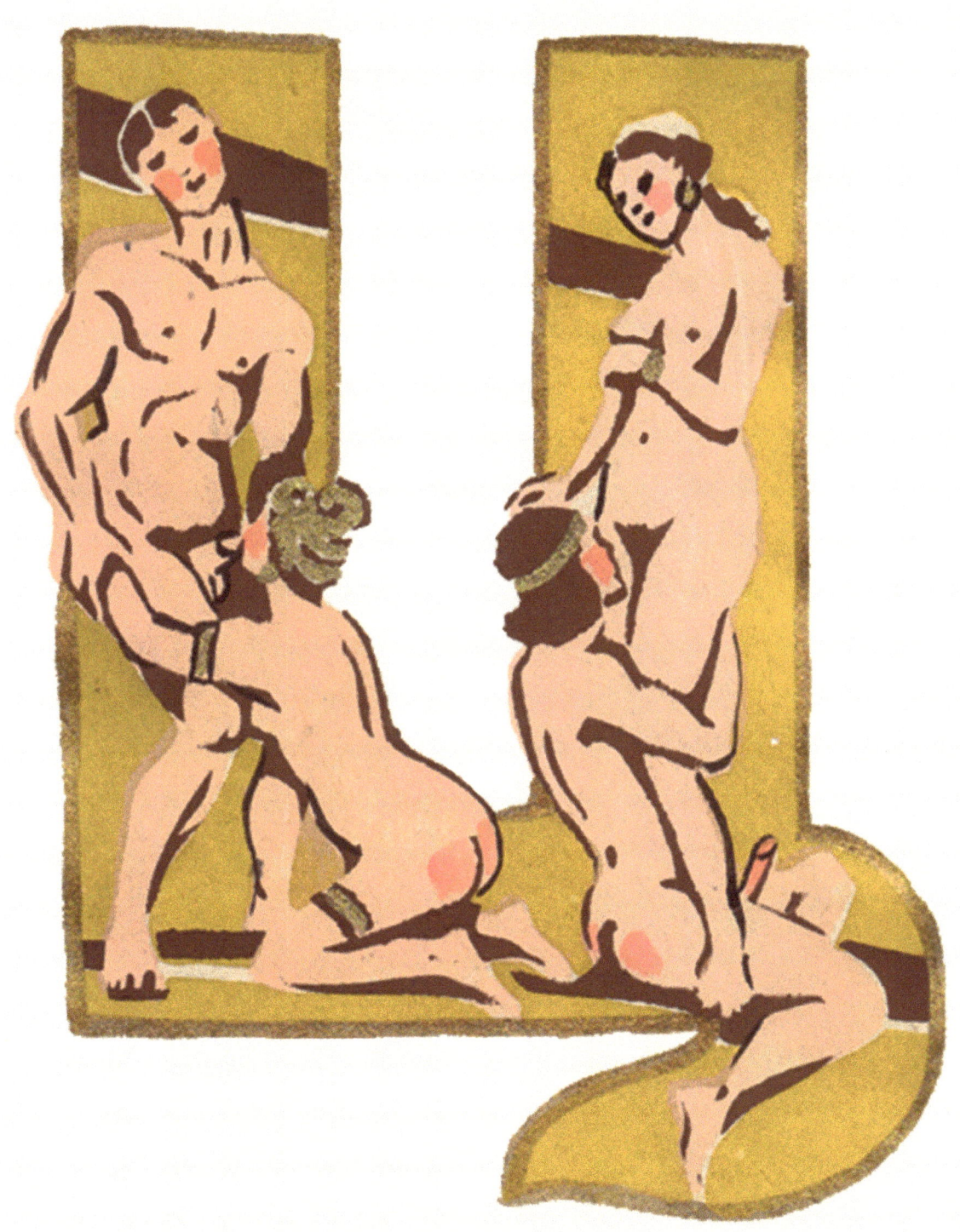

27

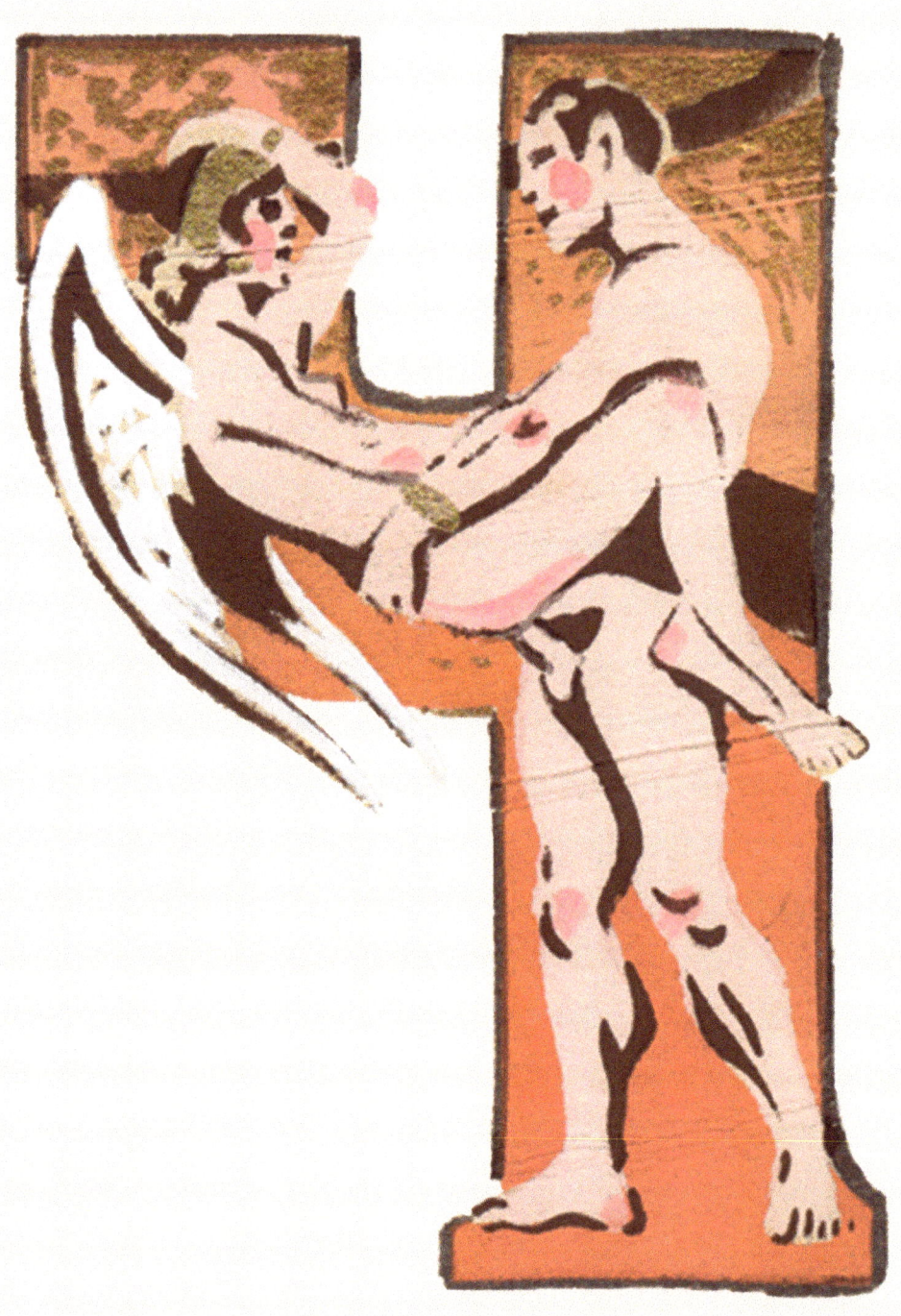

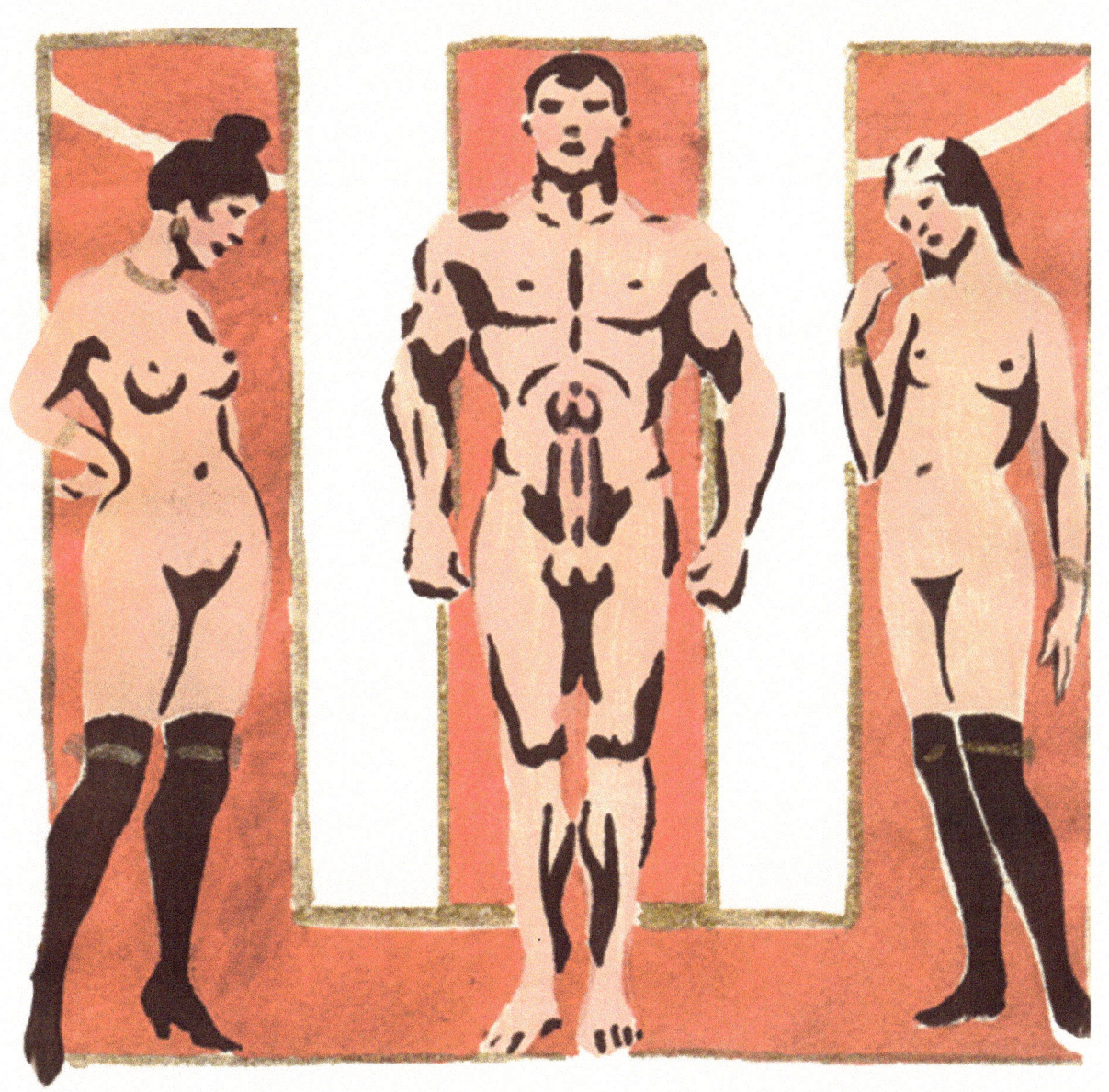

29

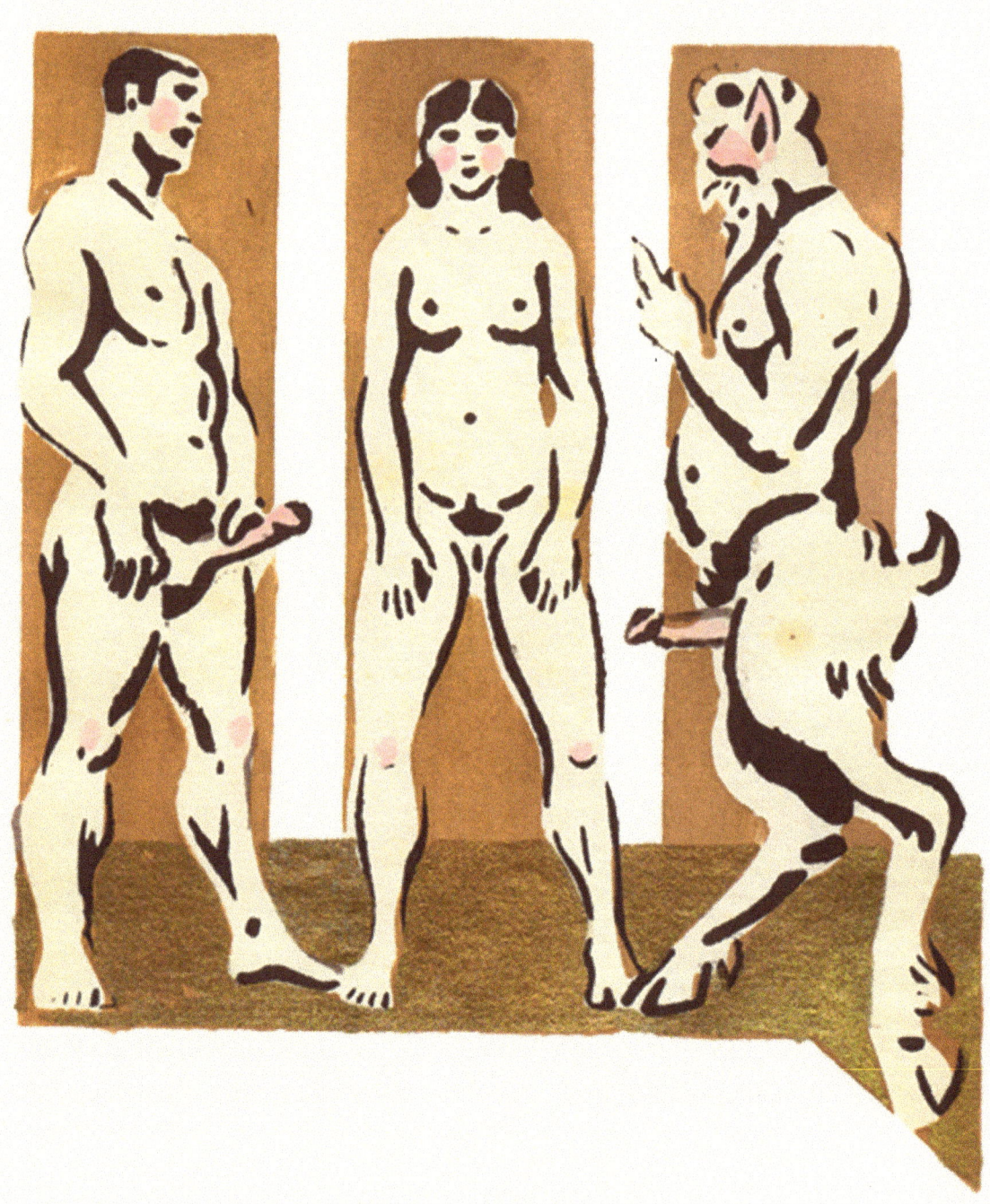

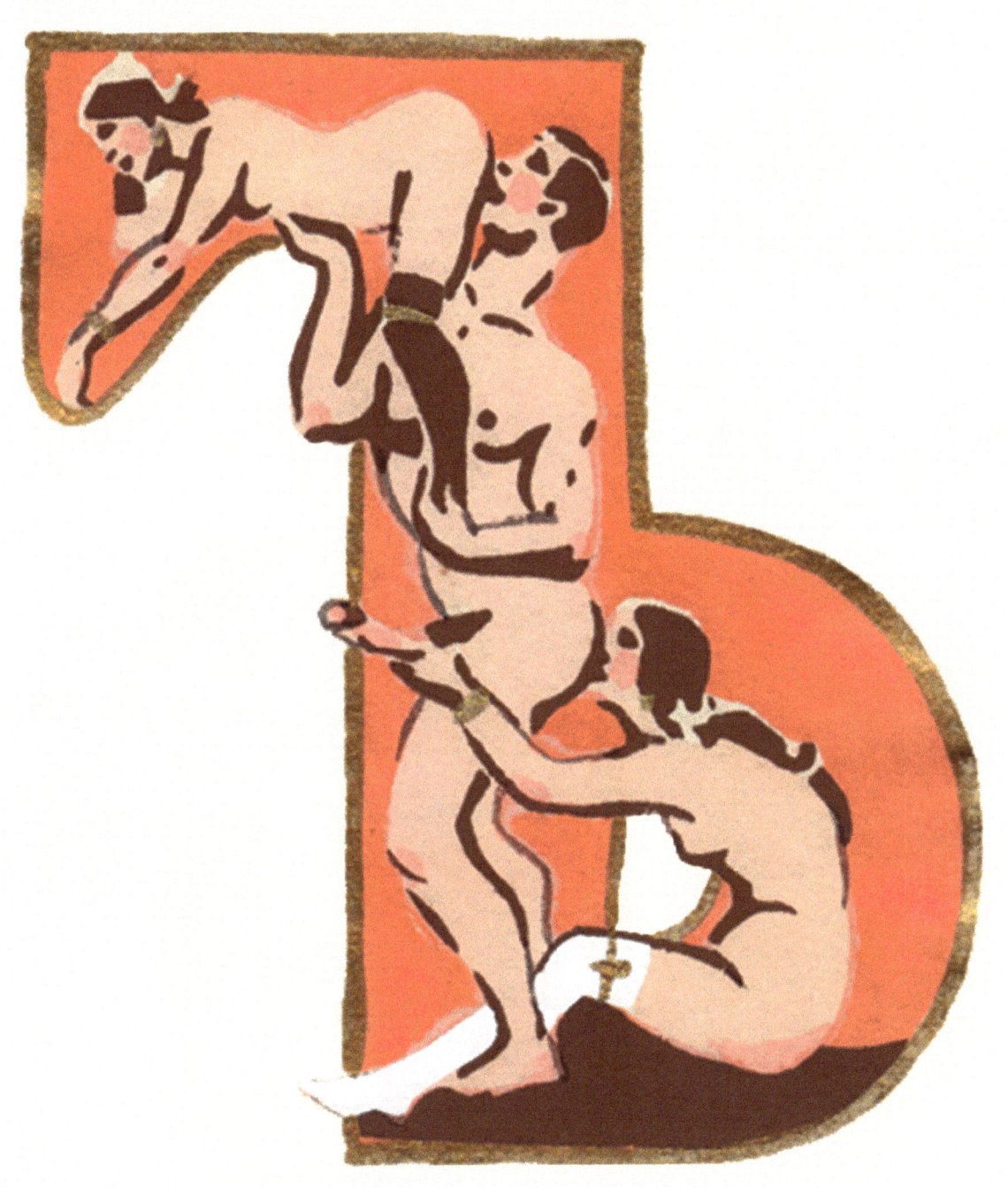

31

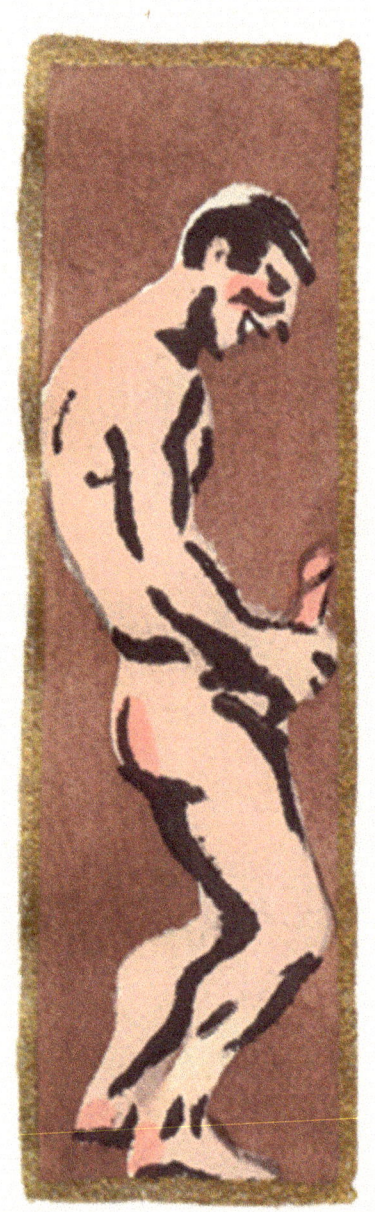

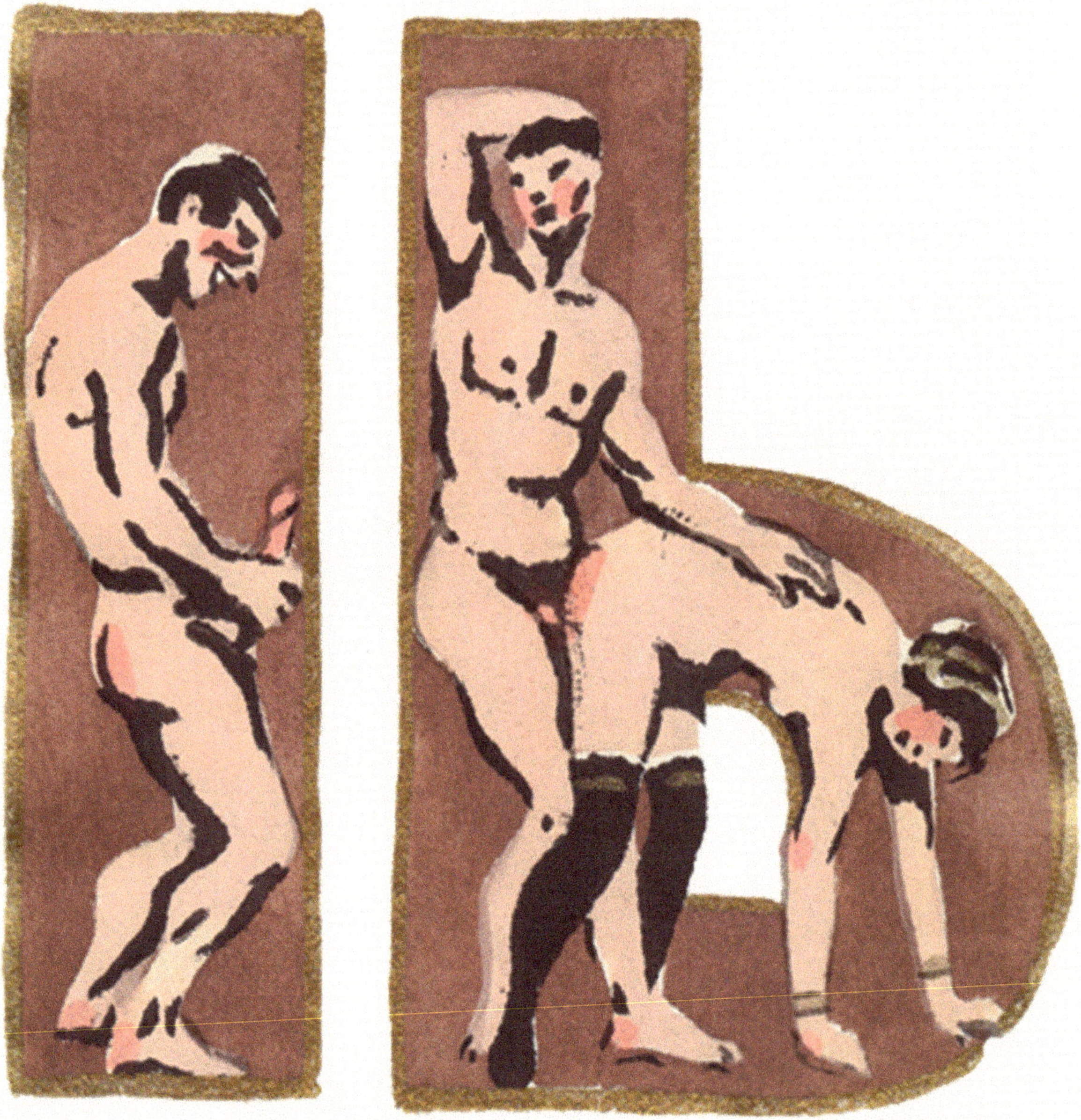

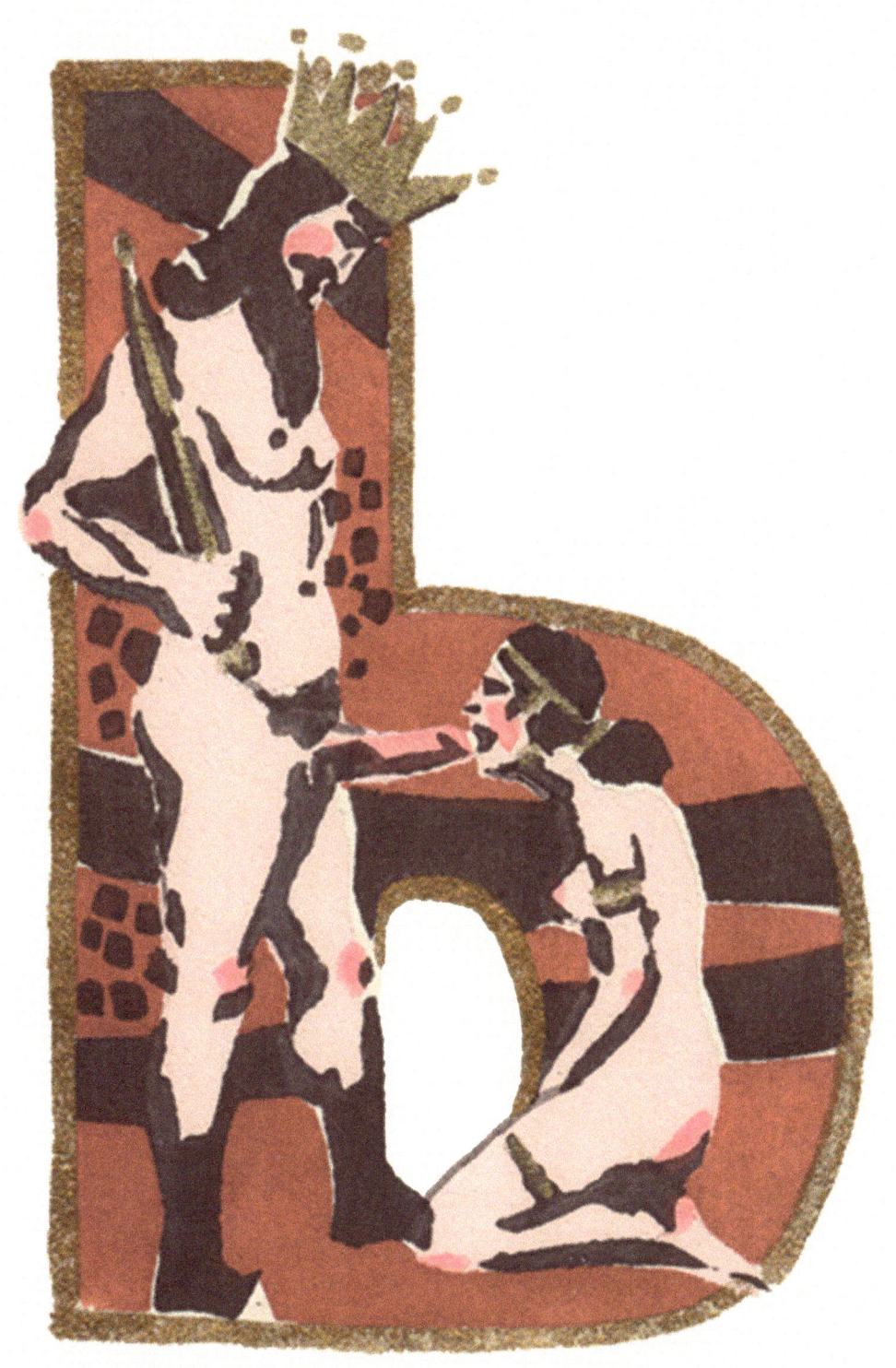

33

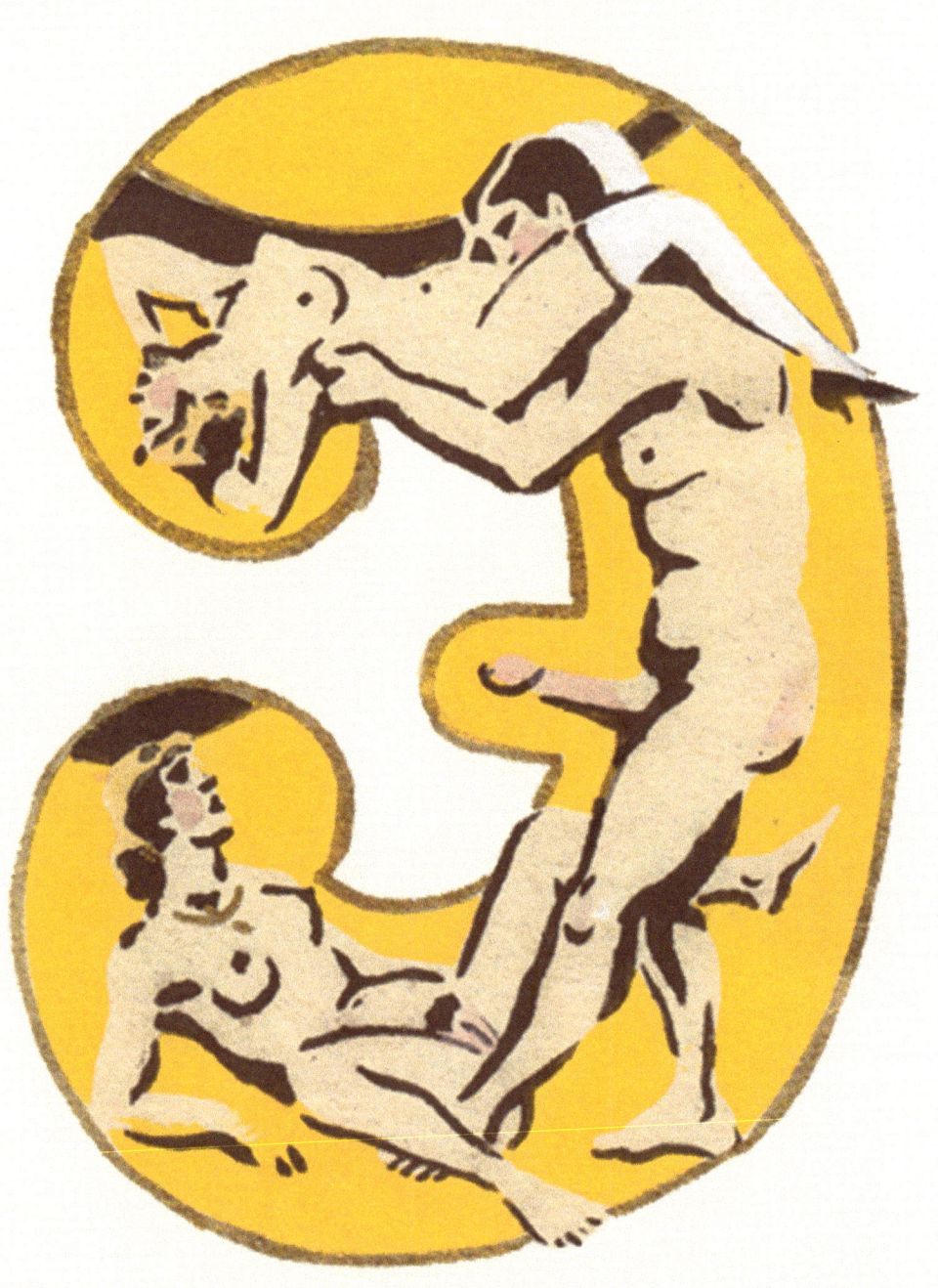

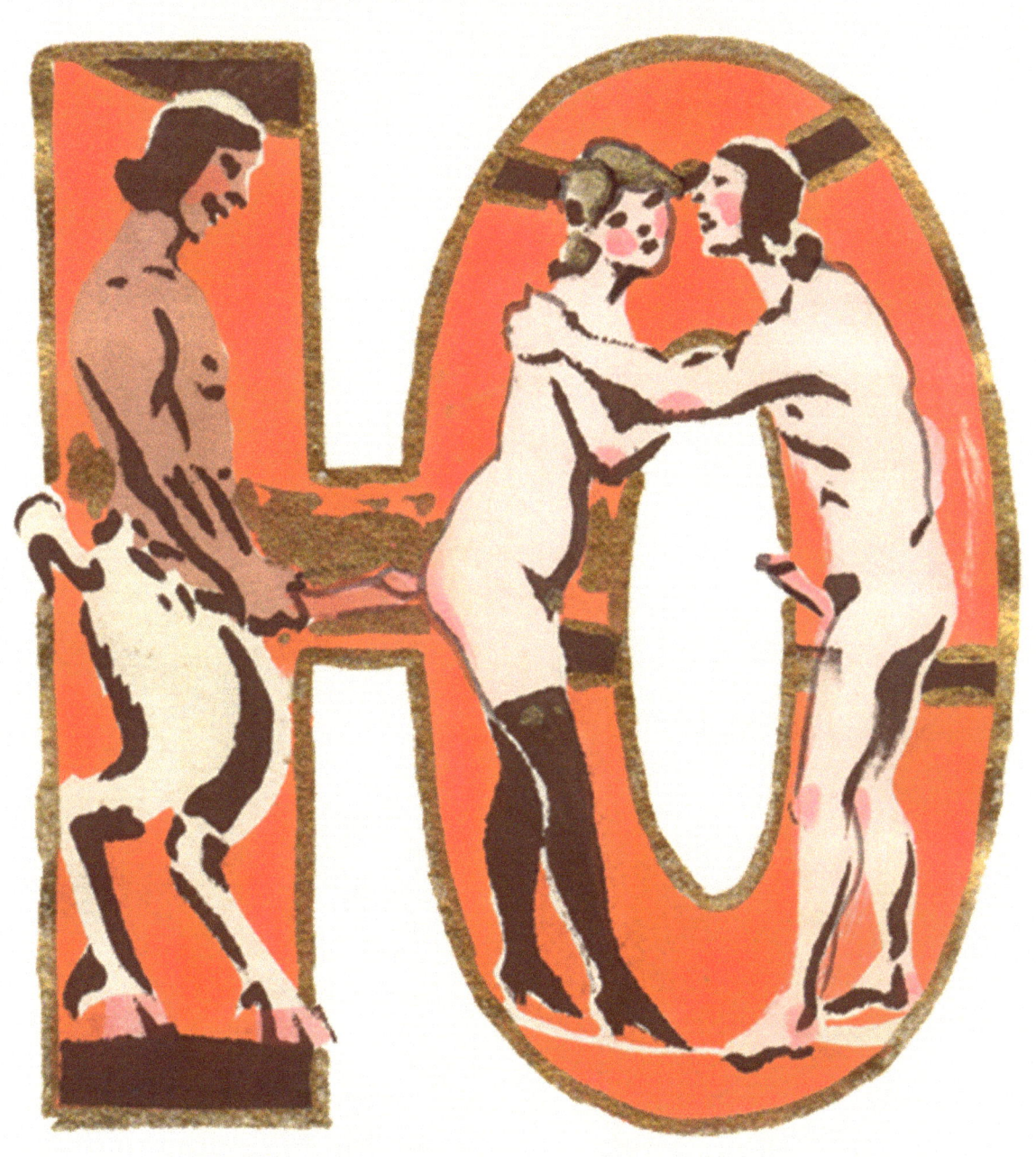

35

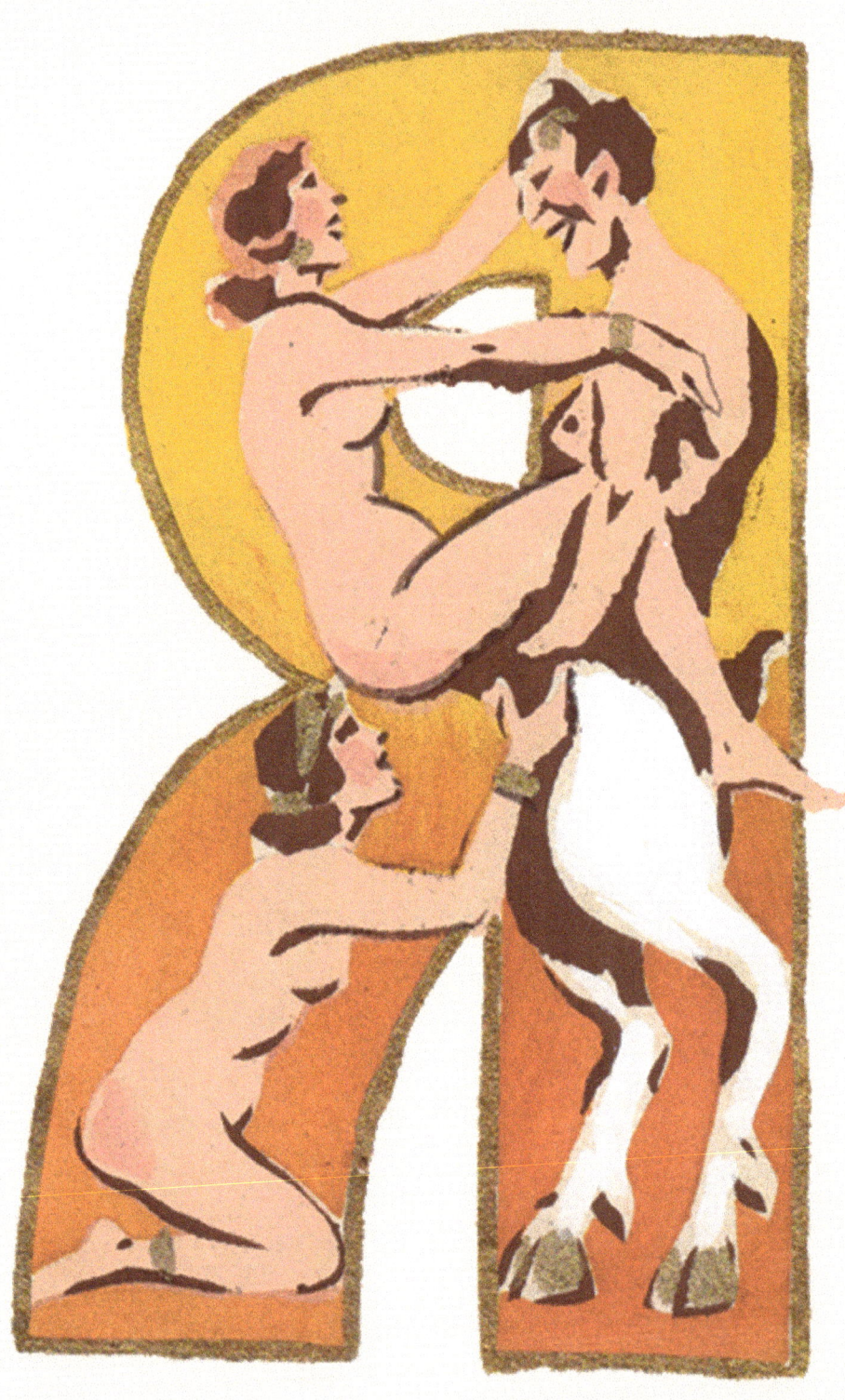

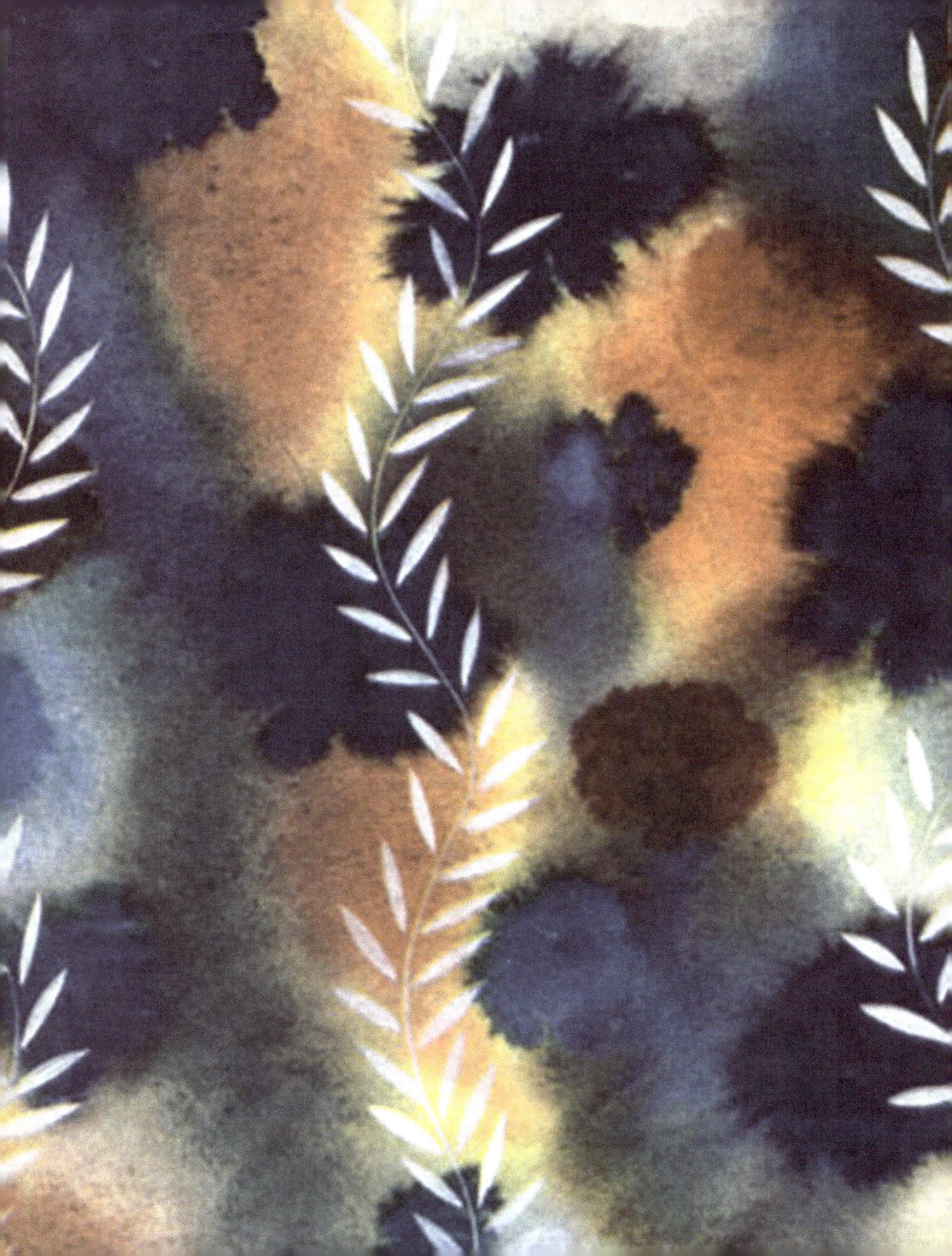

Рисовал С. Д. Меркуров
17 - X - 431 г.

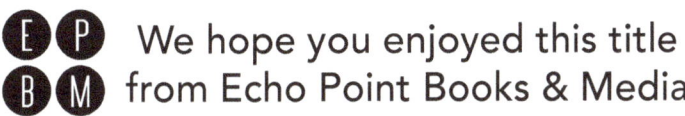 We hope you enjoyed this title
from Echo Point Books & Media

Before Closing this Book, Two Good Things to Know

1. Buy Direct & Save

Go to www.echopointbooks.com (click "Our Titles" at top or click "For Echo Point Publishing" in the middle) to see our complete list of titles. We publish books on a wide variety of topics—from spirituality to auto repair.

Buy direct and save 10% at www.echopointbooks.com

DISCOUNT CODE: EPBUYER

2. Make Literary History and Earn $100 Plus Other Goodies Simply for Your Book Recommendation!

At Echo Point Books & Media we specialize in republishing out-of-print books that are united by one essential ingredient: high quality. Do you know of any great books that are no longer actively published? If so, please let us know. If we end up publishing your recommendation, you'll be adding a wee bit to literary culture and a bunch to our publishing efforts.

Here is how we will thank you:

- A free copy of the new version of your beloved book that includes acknowledgement of your skill as a sharp book scout.
- A free copy of another Echo Point title you like from echopointbooks.com.
- And, oh yes, we'll also send you a check for $100.

Since we publish an eclectic list of titles, we're interested in a wide range of books. So please don't be shy if you have obscure tastes or like books with a practical focus. To get a sense of what kind of books we publish, visit us at www.echopointbooks.com.

If you have a book that you think will work for us,
send us an email at editorial@echopointbooks.com

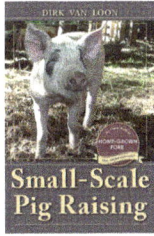 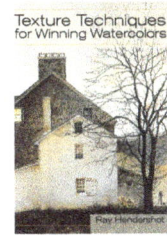 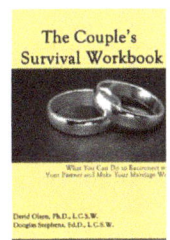 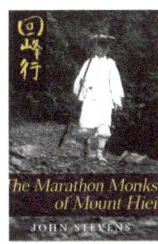 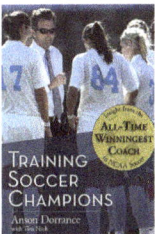

www.ingramcontent.com/pod-product-compliance
Lightning Source LLC
Chambersburg PA
CBHW041921180526
45172CB00013B/1352